INSTANT *Piano Songs*

Audio Access

CHRISTMAS CLASSICS

Simple Sheet Music + Audio Play-Along

T0055740

PLAYBACK+
Speed • Pitch • Balance • Loop

To access audio visit:
www.halleonard.com/mylibrary

Enter Code
6579-4967-6242-6781

ISBN 978-1-5400-9737-8

Visit Hal Leonard Online at
www.halleonard.com

Contact us:
Hal Leonard
7777 West Bluemound Road
Milwaukee, WI 53213
Email: info@halleonard.com

In Europe, contact:
Hal Leonard Europe Limited
42 Wigmore Street
Marylebone, London, W1U 2RN
Email: info@halleonardeurope.com

In Australia, contact:
Hal Leonard Australia Pty. Ltd.
4 Lentara Court
Cheltenham, Victoria, 3192 Australia
Email: info@halleonard.com.au

CONTENTS

Welcome to the *INSTANT Piano Songs* series!

This unique, flexible collection allows you to play with either one hand or two. Three playing options are available—all of which sound great with the online backing tracks:

1. **Play only the melody with your right hand.**

2. **Add basic chords in your left hand, which are notated for you.**

3. **Use suggested rhythm patterns for the left-hand chords.**

Letter names appear inside the notes in both hands to assist you, and there are no key signatures to worry about. If a **sharp** ♯ or **flat** ♭ is needed, it is shown beside the note each time, even within the same measure.

If two notes are connected by a **tie** ‿, hold the first note for the combined number of beats. (The second note does not show a letter name since it is not re-struck.)

Sometimes the melody needs to be played an octave higher to avoid overlapping with the left-hand chords. (If your starting note is C, the next C to the right is one octave higher.) If you are using only your right hand, however, you can disregard this instruction in the music.

🔊 The backing tracks are designed to enhance the piano arrangements, regardless of how you choose to play them. Each track includes two measures of count-off clicks at the beginning. If the recording is too fast or too slow, use the online ***PLAYBACK+*** player to adjust it to a more comfortable tempo (speed).

Optional left-hand rhythm patterns are provided for when you are ready to move beyond the basic chords. The patterns are based on the three notes of the basic chords and appear as small, gray notes in the first line of each song. Feel free to use the suggested pattern throughout the song, or create your own. Sample rhythm patterns are shown below. (Of course, you can always play just the basic chords if you wish!)

Have fun! Whether you play with one hand or two, you'll sound great!

Sample Rhythm Patterns

4/4 Meter

3/4 Meter

6/8 Meter

Also Available

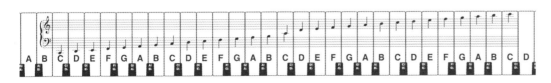
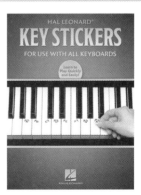

Hal Leonard Student Keyboard Guide HL00296039

Key Stickers HL00100016

Angels We Have Heard on High

Traditional French Carol
Translated by James Chadwick

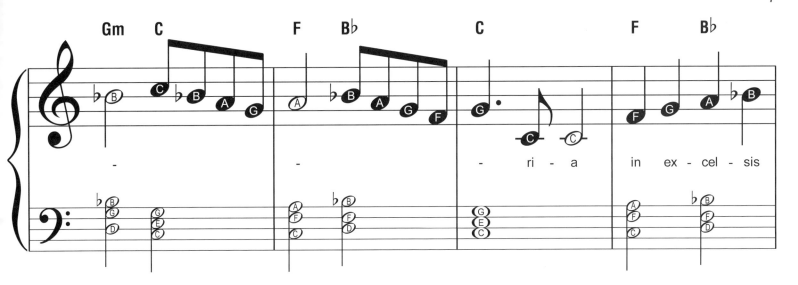

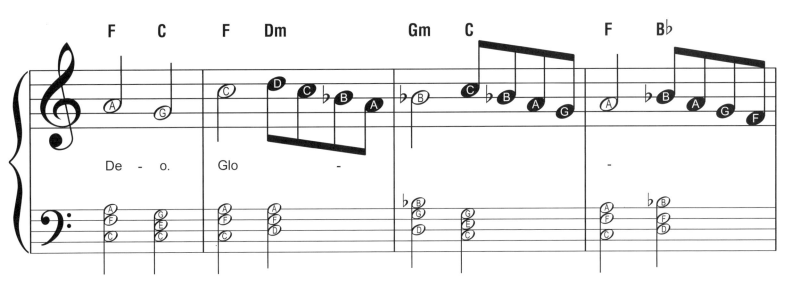

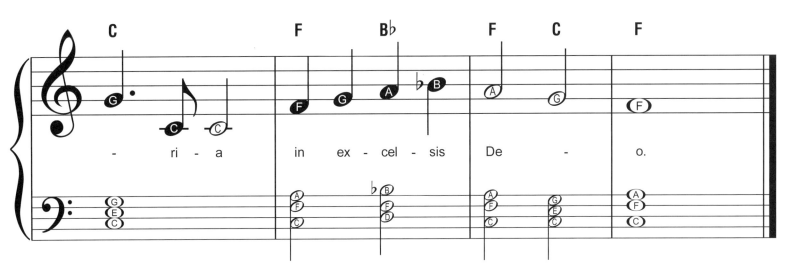

Additional Lyrics

3. Come to Bethlehem and see
   Him whose birth the angels sing.
   Come adore on bended knee
   Christ, the Lord, the newborn King.
   Refrain

4. See within a manger laid
   Jesus, Lord of heav'n and earth.
   Mary, Joseph, lend your aid,
   With us sing our Savior's birth.
   Refrain

Away in a Manger

Words by John T. McFarland (v.3)
Music by James R. Murray

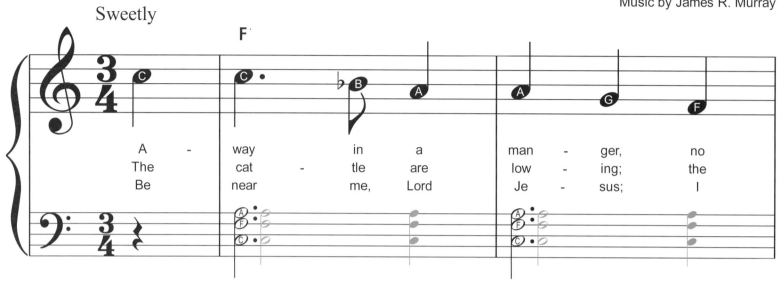

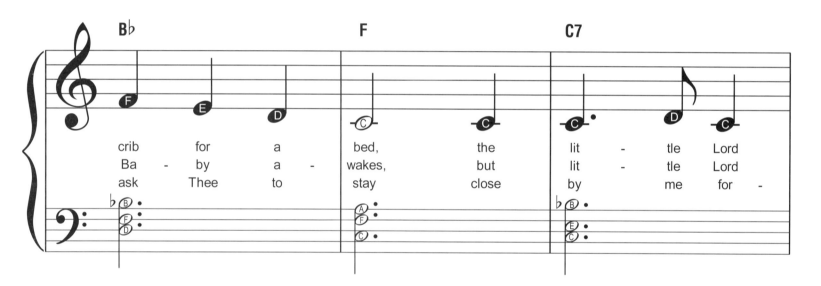

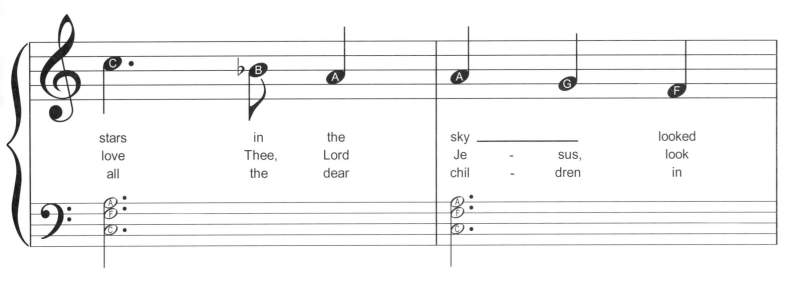

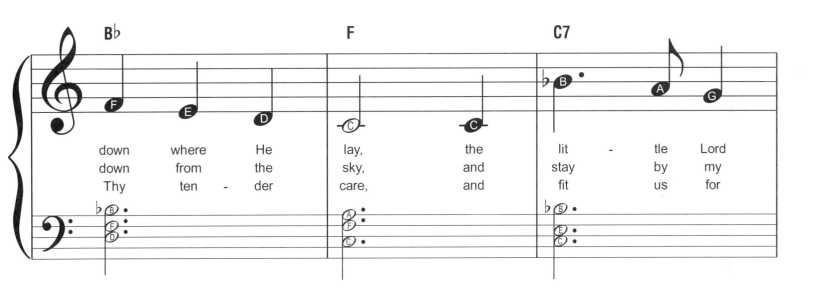

stars in the sky looked
love Thee, Lord Je - sus, look
all the dear chil - dren in
B♭
F
C7
down where He lay, the lit - tle Lord
down from the sky, and stay by my
Thy ten - der care, and fit us for
F
C7
F
Je - sus a - sleep on the hay.
cra - dle 'til morn - ing is nigh.
heav - en to live with Thee there.

Deck the Hall

Traditional Welsh Carol

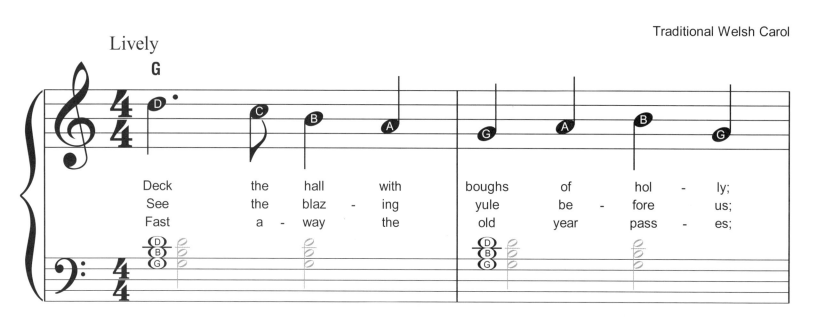

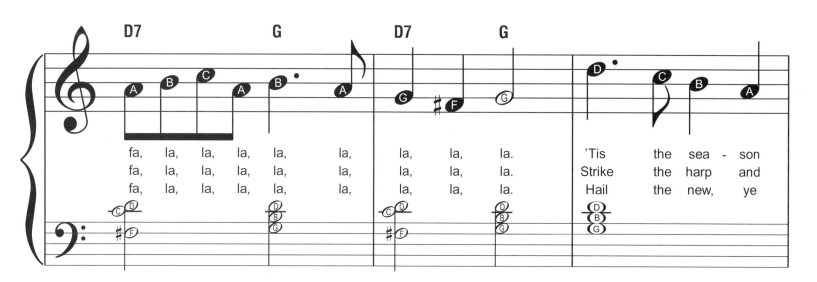

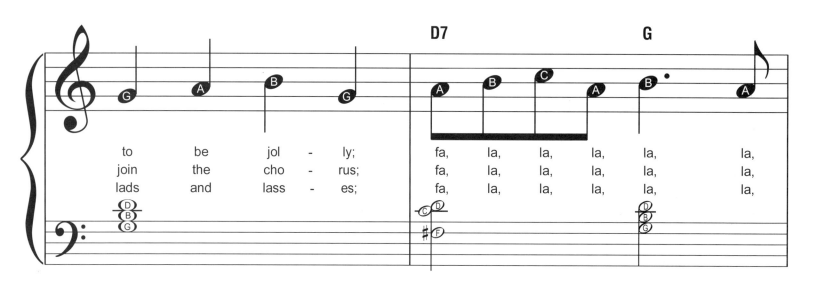

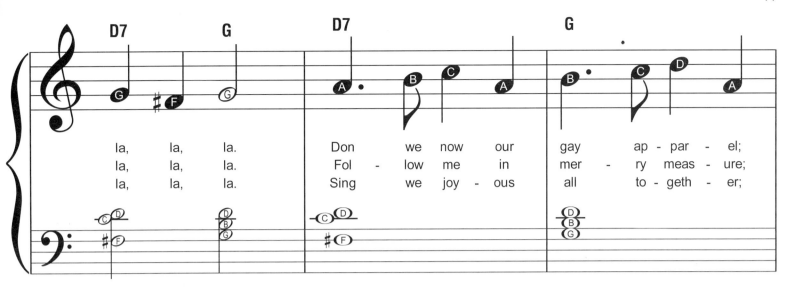

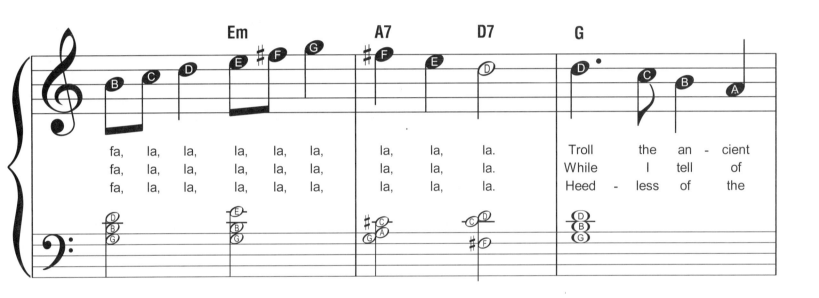

The First Noël

17th Century English Carol
Music from W. Sandys' *Christmas Carols*

Moderately

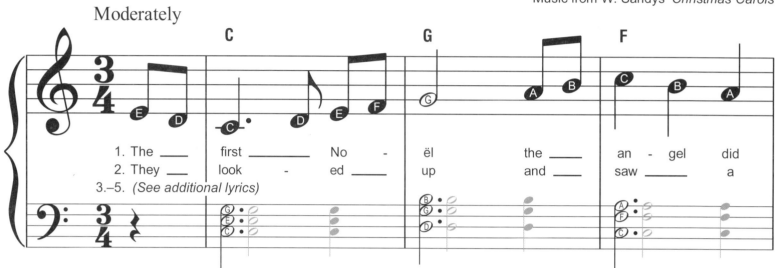

1. The ____ first _____ No - ël ____ the ____ an - gel did
2. They ____ look - ed ____ up and ____ saw _____ a

3.–5. *(See additional lyrics)*

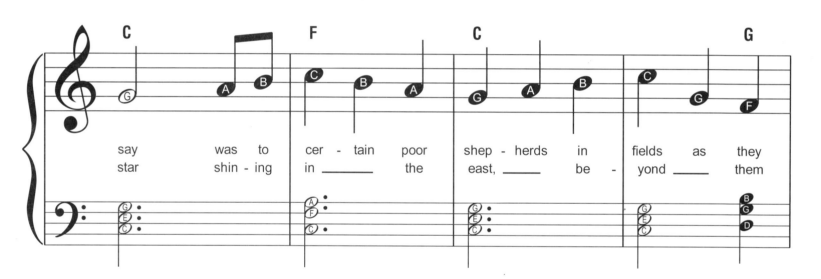

say was to cer - tain poor shep - herds in fields as they
star shin - ing in ____ the east, ____ be - yond ____ them

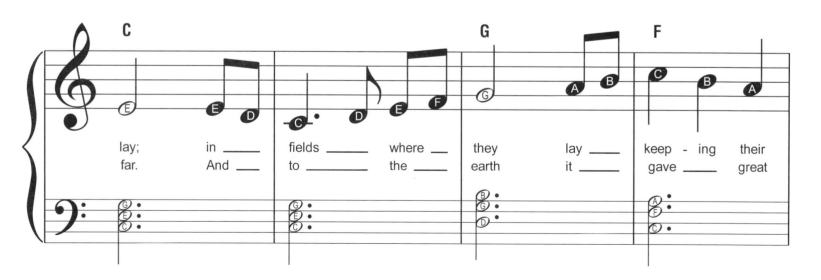

lay; in ____ fields ____ where ____ they lay ____ keep - ing their
far. And ____ to ____ the ____ earth it ____ gave ____ great

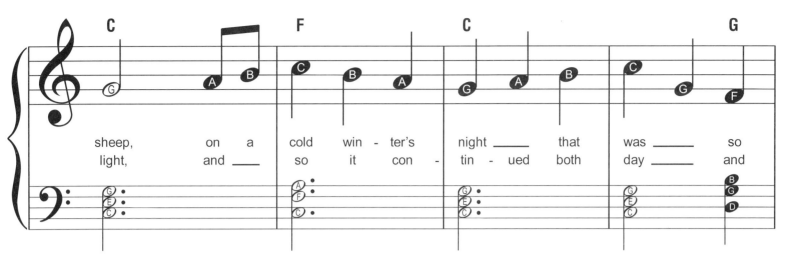

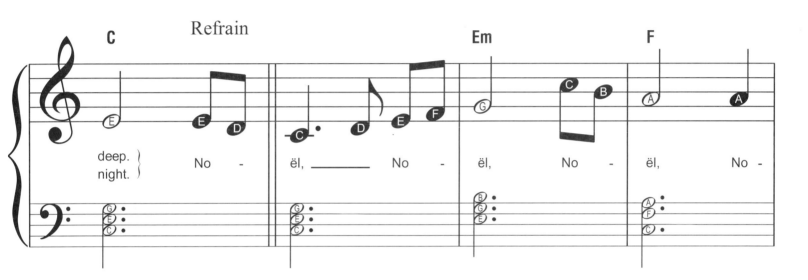

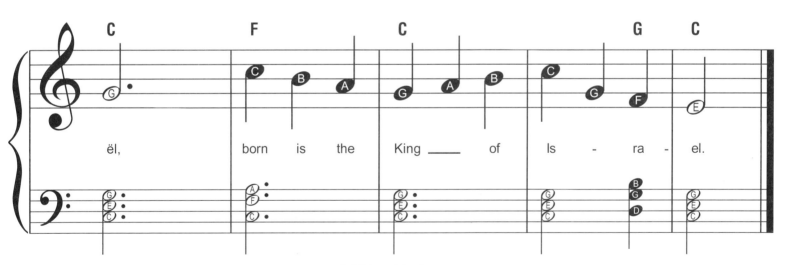

Additional Lyrics

3. And by the light of that same star,
Three wise men came from country far;
To seek for a King was their intent,
And to follow the star wherever it went.
Refrain

4. This star drew nigh to the northwest,
O'er Bethlehem it took its rest;
And there it did both stop and stay,
Right over the place where Jesus lay.
Refrain

5. Then entered in those wise men three,
Full reverently upon their knee;
And offered there in His presence,
Their gold and myrrh and frankincense.
Refrain

Go, Tell It on the Mountain

African-American Spiritual
Verses by John W. Work, Jr.

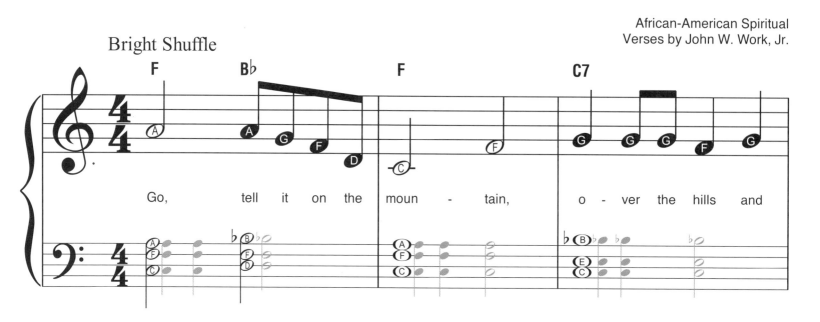

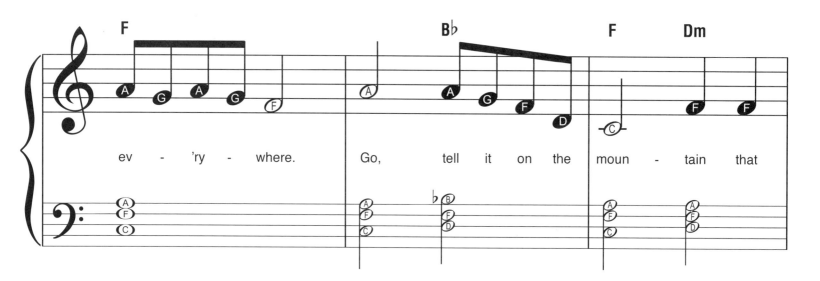

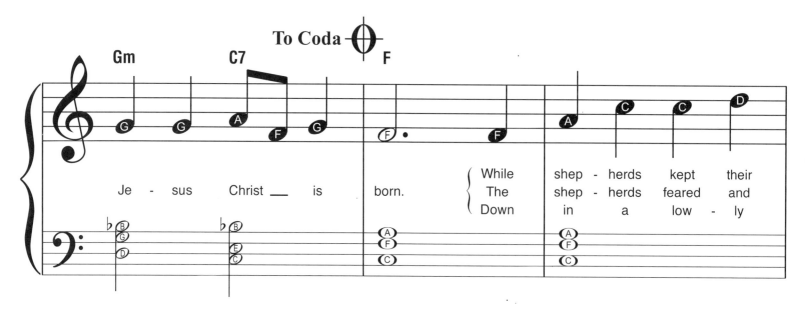

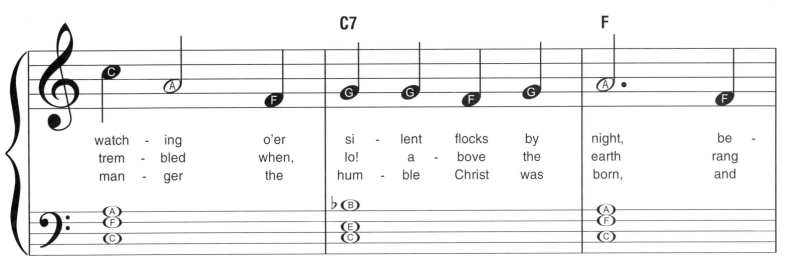

watch - ing o'er
trem - bled when,
man - ger the

si - lent flocks by
lo! a - bove the
hum - ble Christ was

night, be -
earth born,
born, and

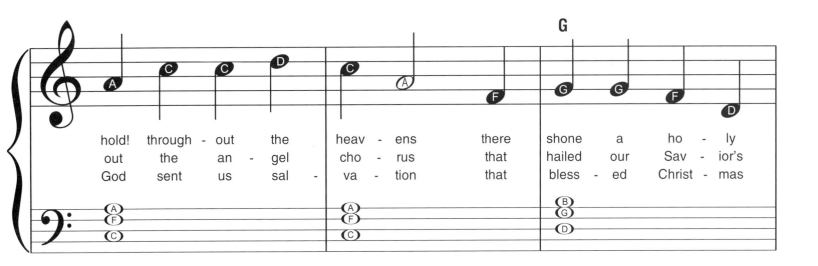

hold! through - out the
out the an - gel
God sent us sal -

heav - ens there
cho - rus that
va - tion that

shone a ho - ly
hailed our Sav - ior's
bless - ed Christ - mas

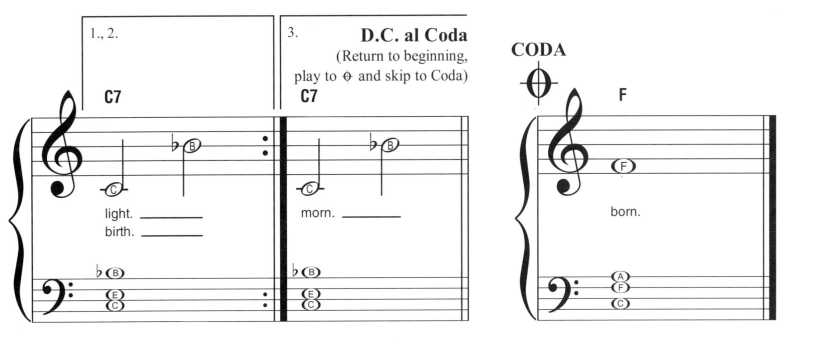

1., 2.

3. **D.C. al Coda**
(Return to beginning,
play to ⊕ and skip to Coda)

CODA

light. _____
birth. _____

morn. _____

born.

God Rest Ye Merry, Gentlemen

Traditional English Carol

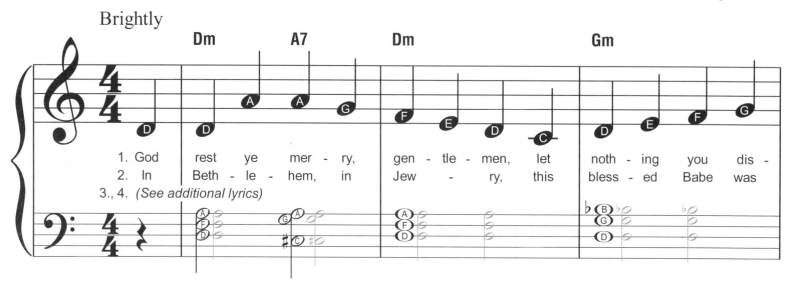

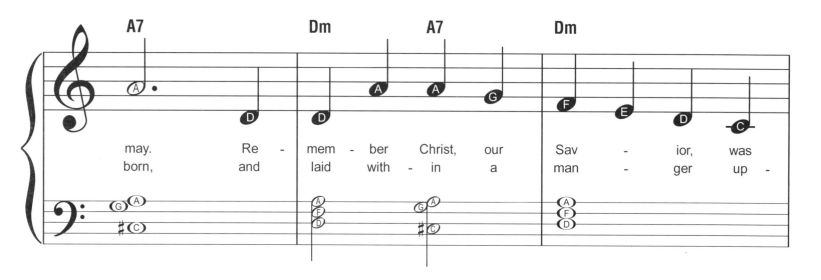

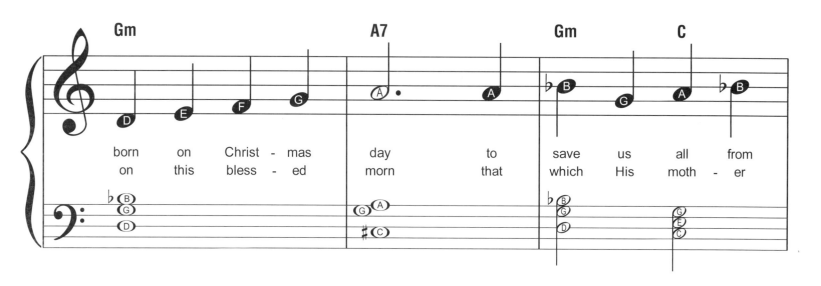

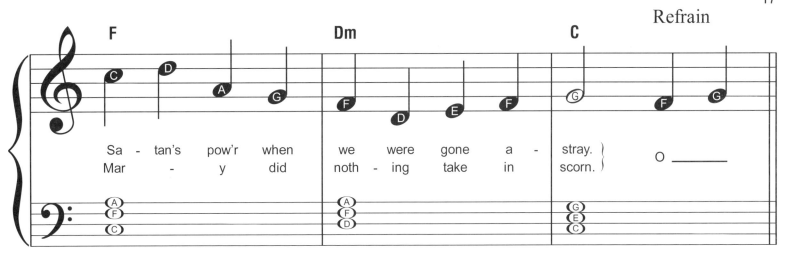

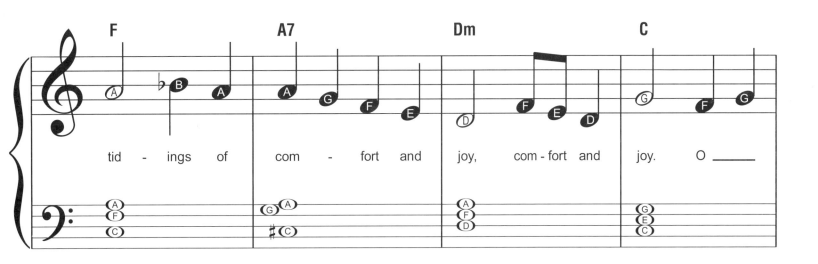

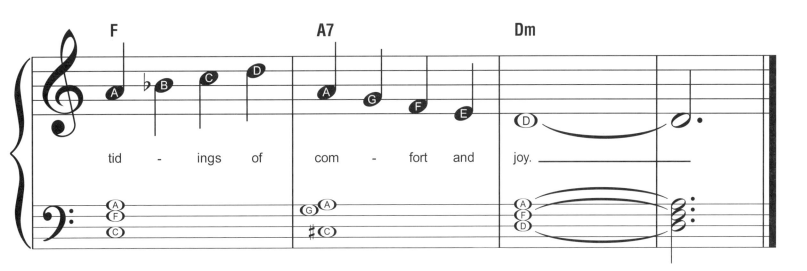

Additional Lyrics

3. From God, our heav'nly Father, a blessed angel came,
And unto certain shepherds brought tidings of the same;
How that in Bethlehem was born the Son of God by name.
Refrain

4. Now shepherds at those tidings rejoiced much in mind,
And left their flocks afeeding in tempest, storm and wind,
And went to Bethlehem straightway, the Son of God to find.
Refrain

Good King Wenceslas

Words by John M. Neale
Music from *Piae Cantiones*

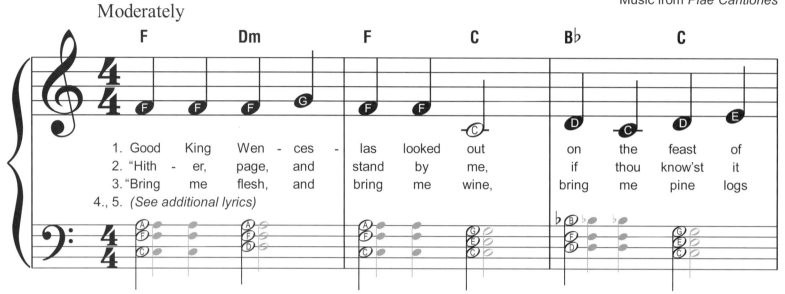

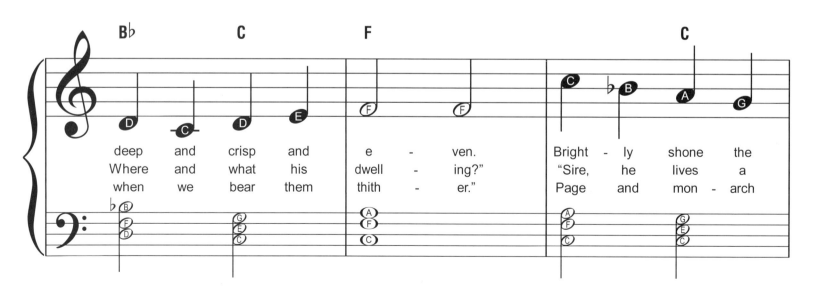

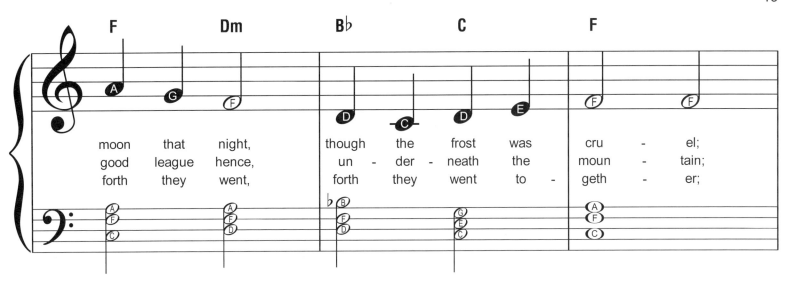

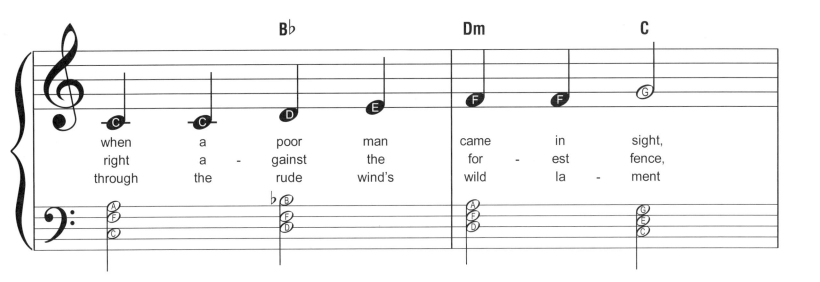

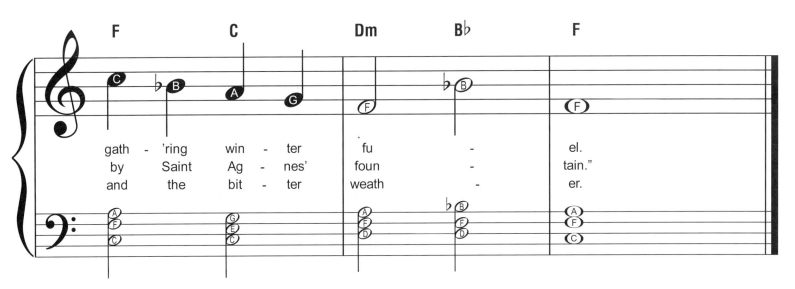

Additional Lyrics

4. "Sire, the night is darker now,
   And the wind blows stronger;
   Fails my heart, I know not how,
   I can go no longer."
   "Mark my footsteps, my good page,
   Tread thou in them boldly;
   Thou shalt find the winter's rage
   Freeze thy blood less coldly."

5. In his master's steps he trod,
   Where the snow lay dinted;
   Heat was in the very sod
   Which the saint has printed.
   Therefore, Christian men, be sure,
   Wealth or rank possessing;
   Ye who now will bless the poor
   Shall yourselves find blessing.

Hark! The Herald Angels Sing

Words by Charles Wesley
Altered by George Whitefield
Music by Felix Mendelssohn-Bartholdy
Arranged by William H. Cummings

Moderately

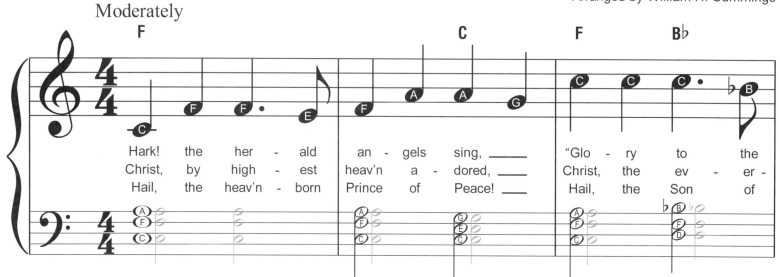

Hark! the her - ald an - gels sing, ___ "Glo - ry to the
Christ, by high - est heav'n a - dored, ___ Christ, the ev - er -
Hail, the heav'n - born Prince of Peace! ___ Hail, the Son of

new - born King! Peace on earth, and mer - cy mild, ___
last - ing Lord! Late in time be - hold Him come, ___
right - eous - ness! Light and life to all He brings, ___

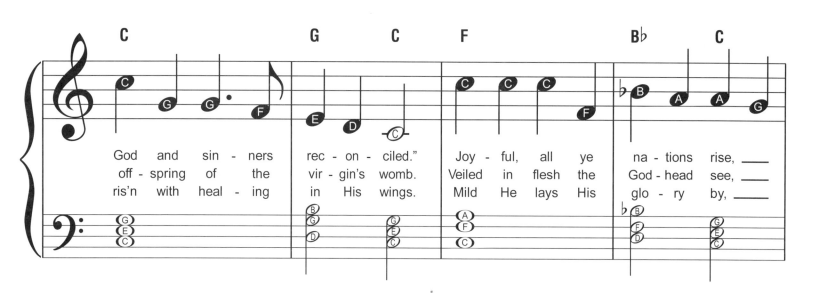

God and sin - ners rec - on - ciled." Joy - ful, all ye na - tions rise, ___
off - spring of the vir - gin's womb. Veiled in flesh the God - head see, ___
ris'n with heal - ing in His wings. Mild He lays His glo - ry by, ___

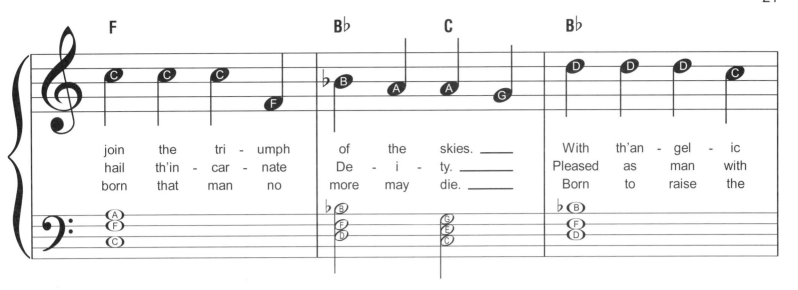

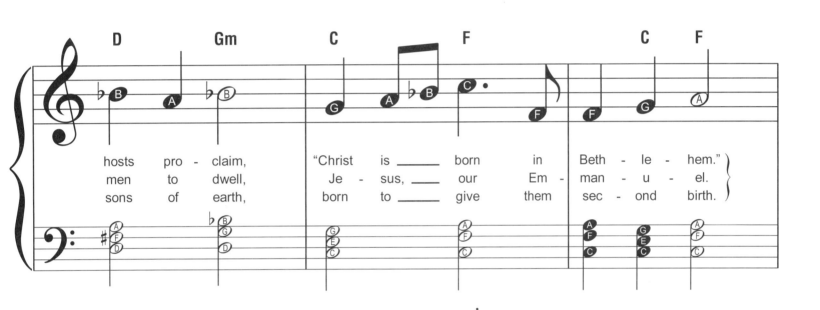

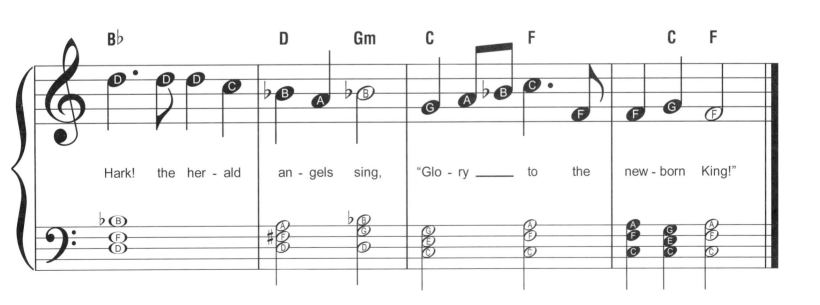

The Holly and the Ivy

18th Century English Carol

Moderately slow

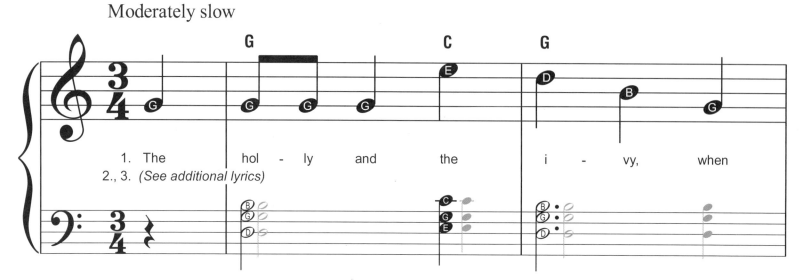

1. The hol - ly and the i - vy, when
2., 3. *(See additional lyrics)*

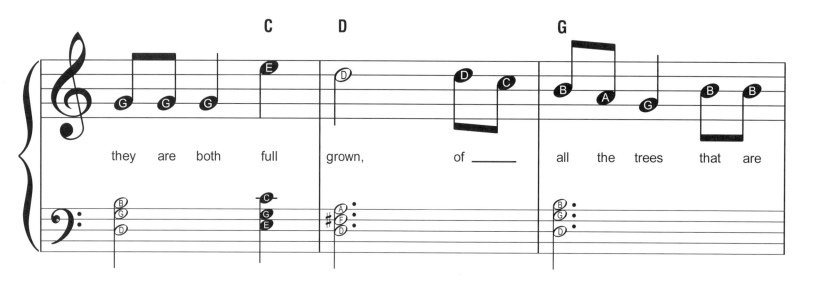

they are both full grown, of _____ all the trees that are

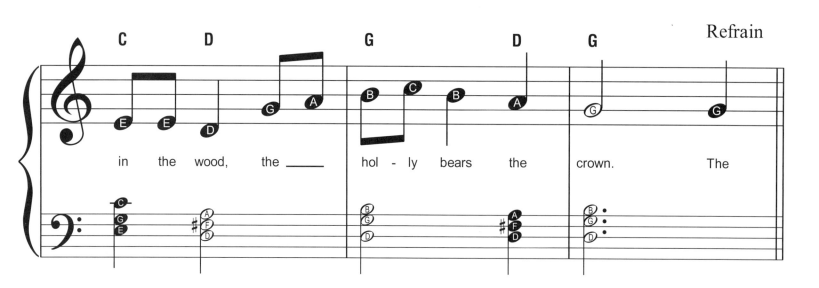

in the wood, the _____ hol - ly bears the crown. The

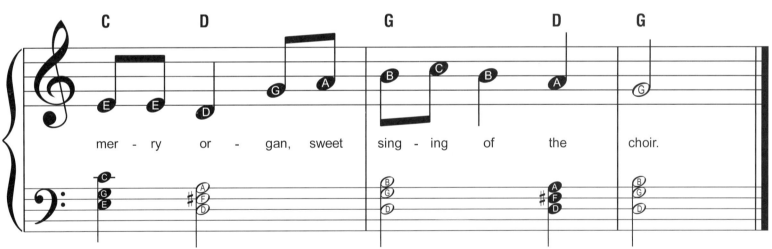

Additional Lyrics

2. The holly bears a blossom
   As white as lily flow'r,
   And Mary bore sweet Jesus Christ
   To be our sweet Savior.
   Refrain

3. The holly bears a berry
   As red as any blood,
   And Mary bore sweet Jesus Christ
   To do poor sinners good.
   Refrain

I Heard the Bells on Christmas Day

Words by Henry Wadsworth Longfellow
Music by John Baptiste Calkin

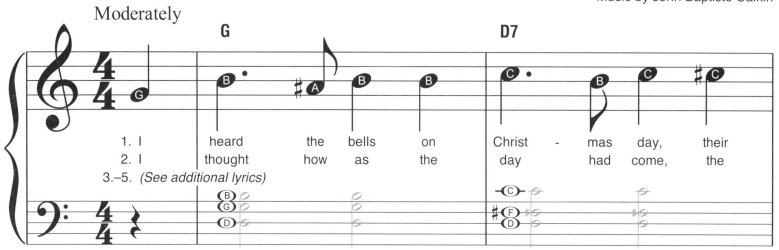

1. I heard the bells on Christ - mas day, their
2. I thought how as on the day had come, the
3.–5. *(See additional lyrics)*

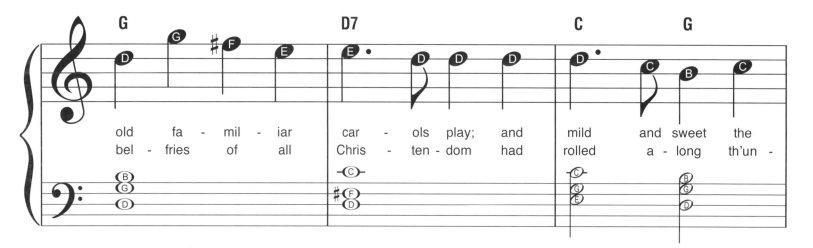

old fa - mil - iar car - ols play; and mild and sweet the
bel - fries of all Chris - ten - dom had rolled a - long th'un -

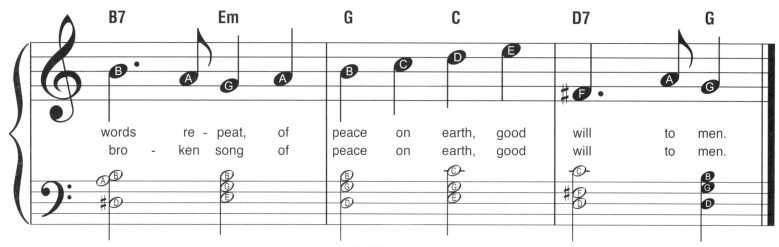

words re - peat, of peace on earth, good will to men.
bro - ken song of peace on earth, good will to men.

Additional Lyrics

3. And in despair I bowed my head:
   "There is no peace on earth," I said,
   "For hate is strong, and mocks the song
   Of peace on earth, good will to men."

4. Then pealed the bells more loud and deep:
   "God is not dead, nor doth He sleep;
   The wrong shall fail, the right prevail,
   With peace on earth, good will to men."

5. Till ringing, singing on its way,
   The world revolved from night to day;
   A voice, a chime, a chant sublime,
   Of peace on earth, good will to men!

Jingle Bells

Words and Music by
J. Pierpont

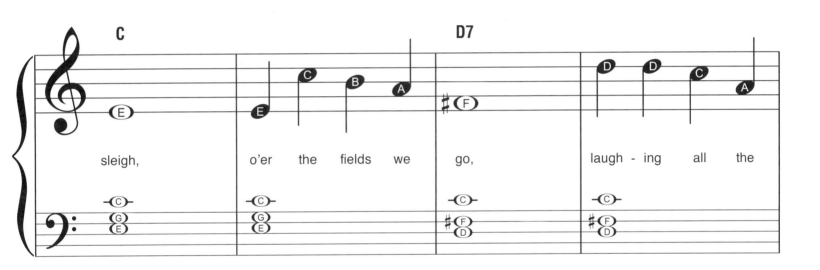

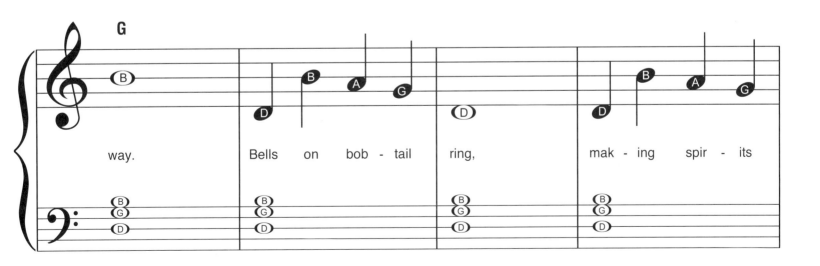

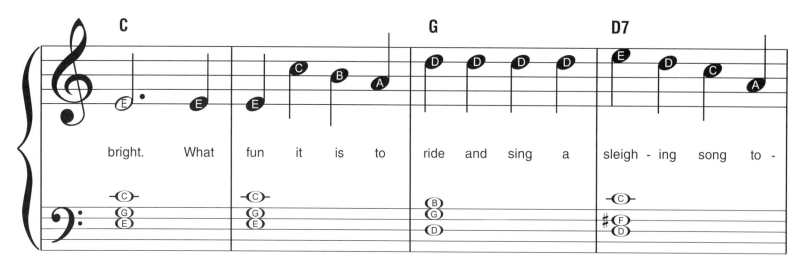

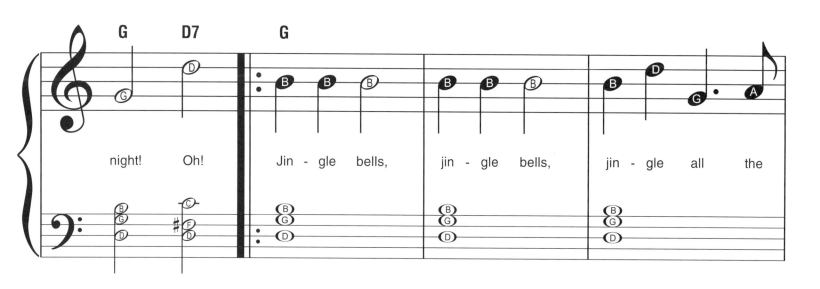

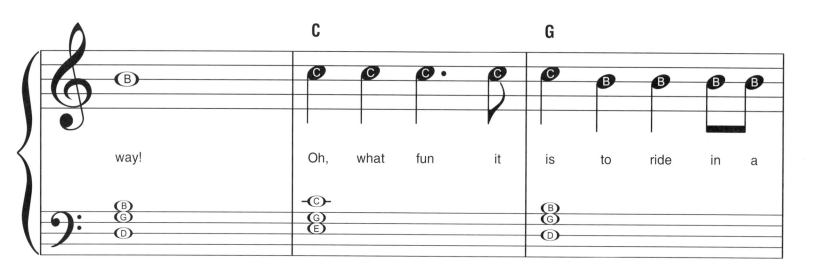

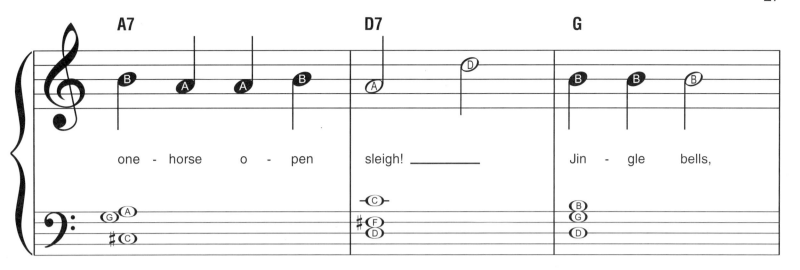

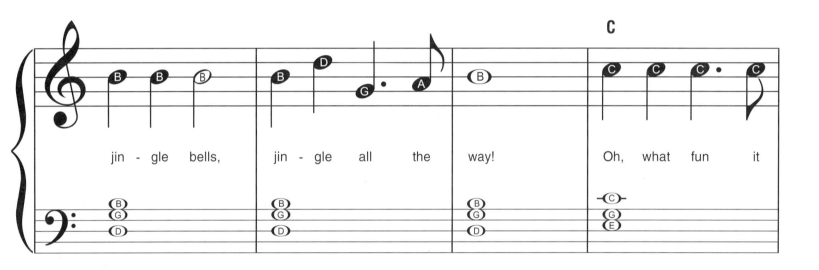

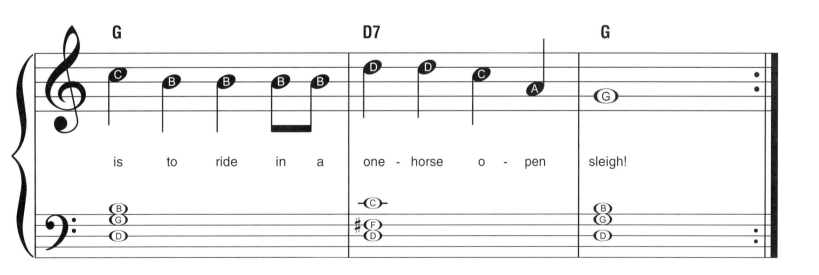

In the Bleak Midwinter

Poem by Christina Rossetti
Music by Gustav Holst

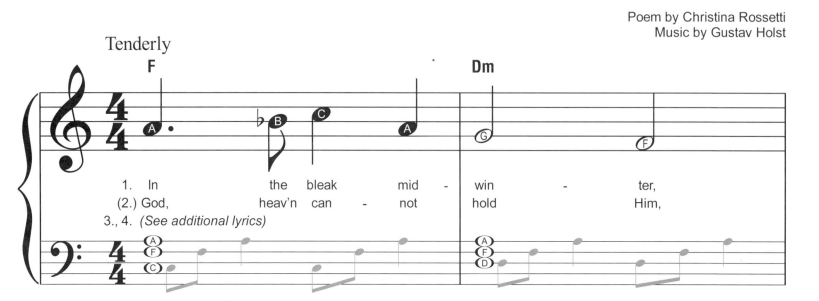

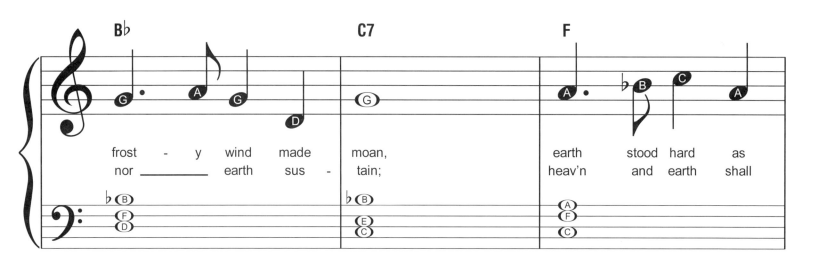

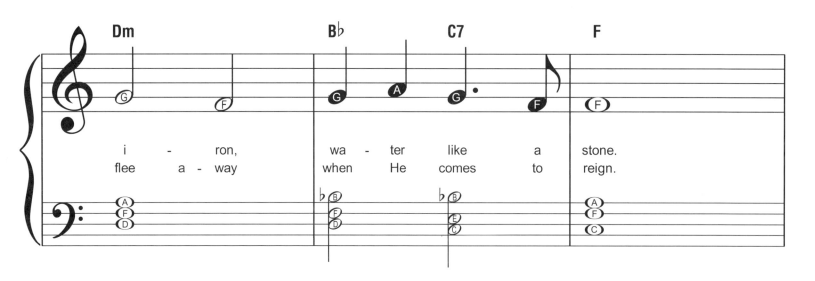

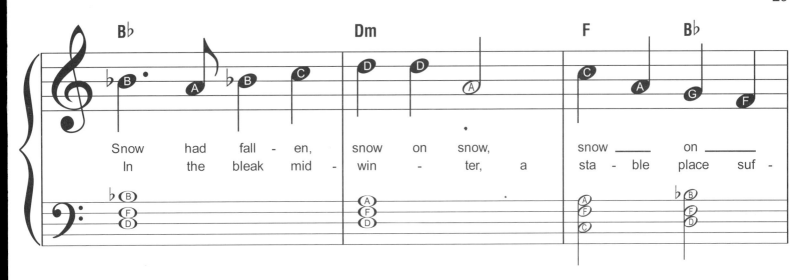

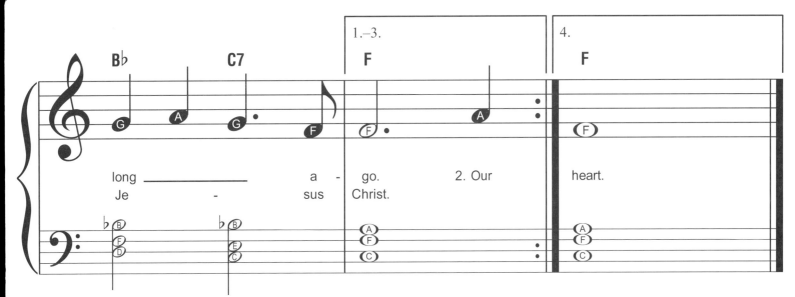

Additional Lyrics

3. Angels and archangels may have gathered there,
   Cherubim and seraphim thronged the air.
   But His mother only, in her maiden bliss,
   Worshiped the Beloved with a kiss.

4. What can I give Him, poor as I am?
   If I were a shepherd, I would bring a lamb.
   If I were a wise man, I would do my part.
   Yet, what can I give Him? Give my heart.

It Came Upon the Midnight Clear

Words by Edmund Hamilton Sears
Music by Richard Storrs Willis

Moderately

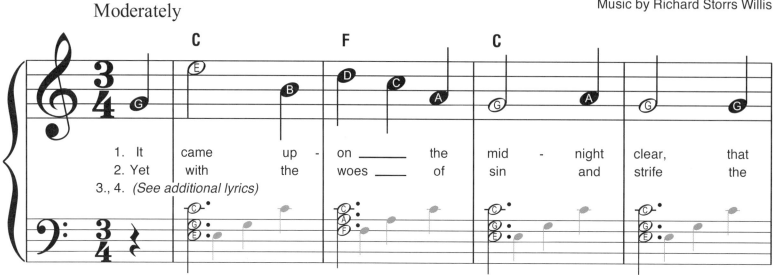

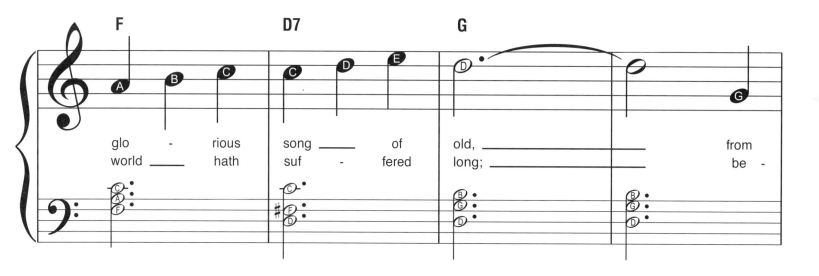

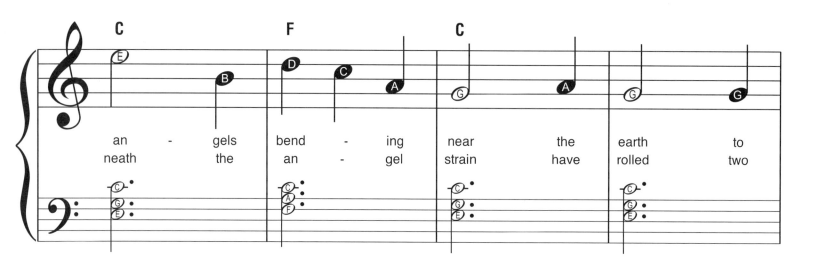

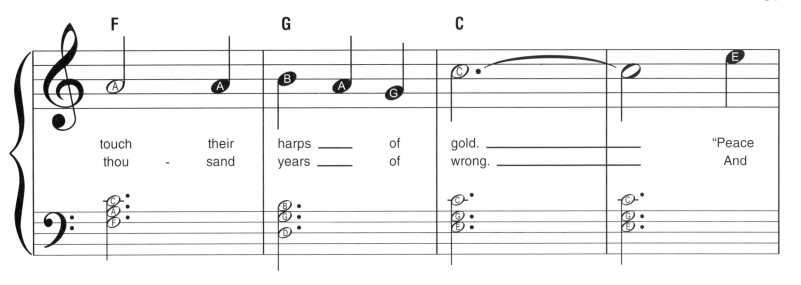

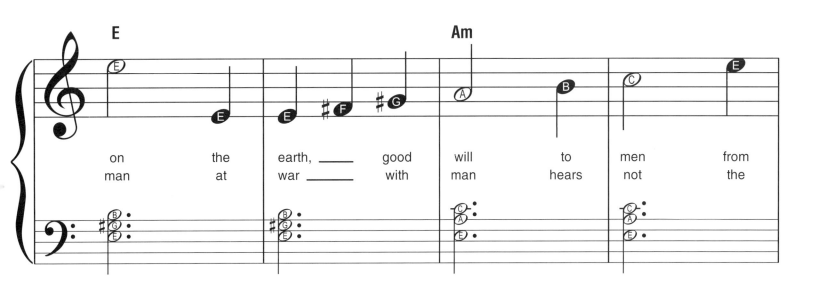

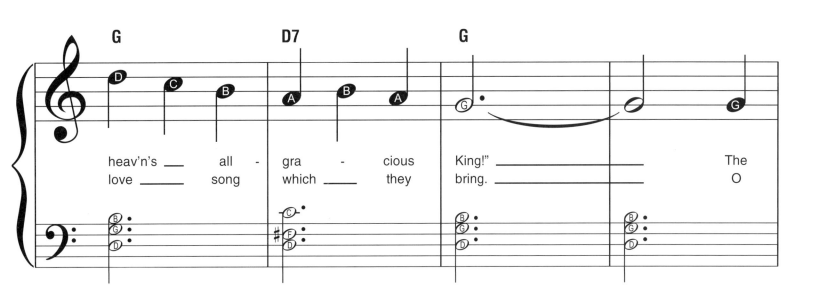

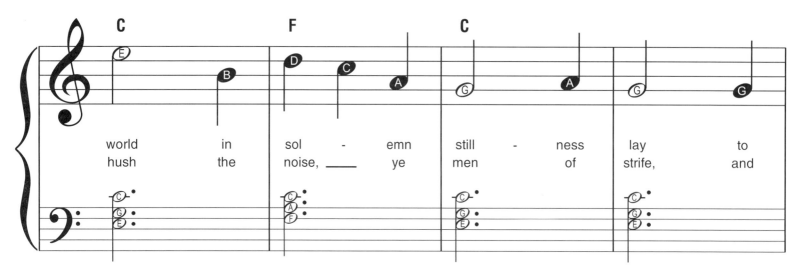

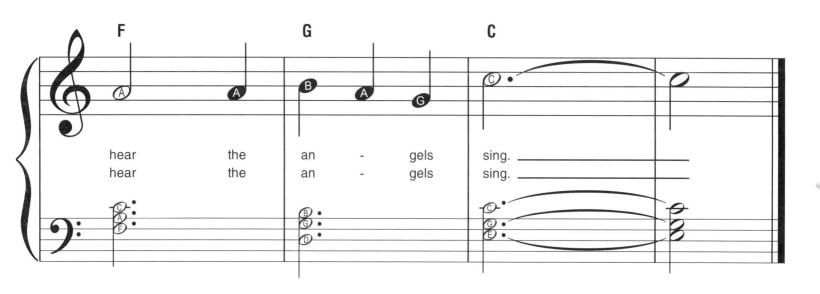

Additional Lyrics

3. And ye, beneath life's crushing load,
   Whose forms are bending low,
   Who toil along the climbing way
   With painful steps and slow;
   Look now, for glad and golden hours
   Come swiftly on the wing.
   O rest beside the weary road
   And hear the angels sing.

4. For lo, the days are hast'ning on,
   By prophet bards foretold,
   When with the ever-circling years
   Comes round the age of gold;
   When peace shall over all the earth
   Its ancient splendors fling,
   And the whole world give back the song
   Which now the angels sing.

O Holy Night

French Words by Placide Cappeau
English Words by John S. Dwight
Music by Adolphe Adam

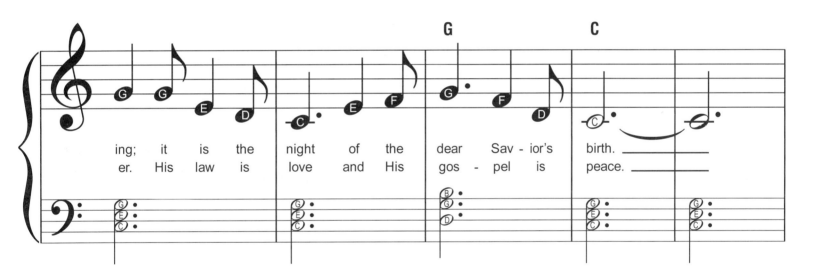

Jolly Old St. Nicholas

Traditional 19th Century American Carol

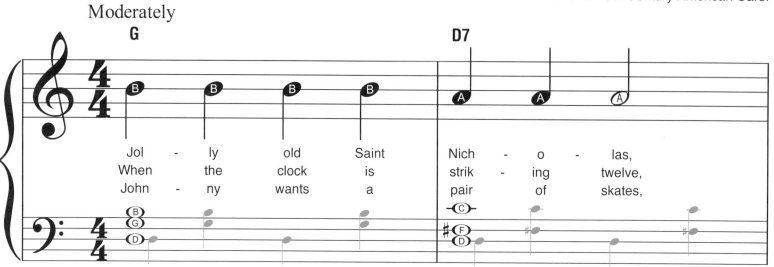

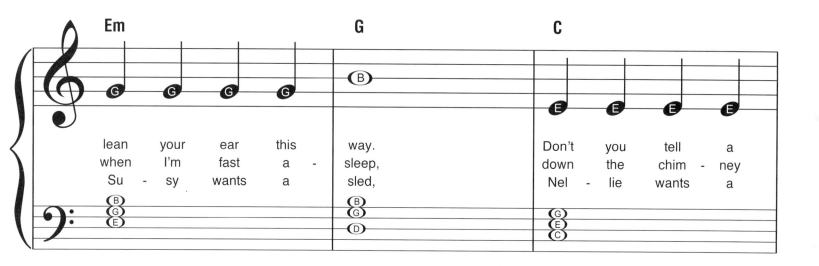

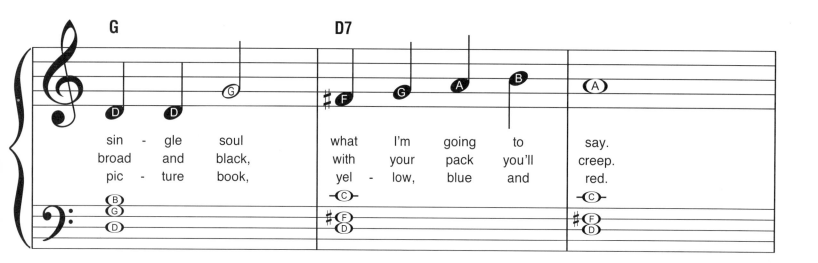

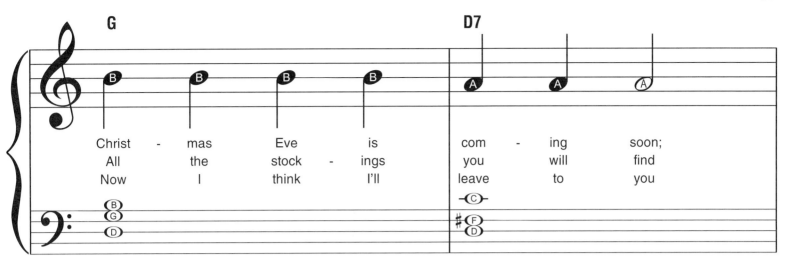

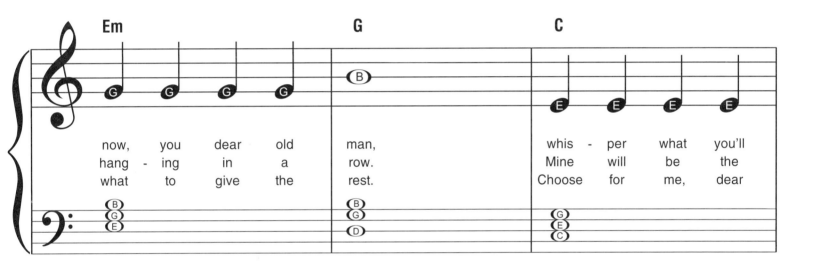

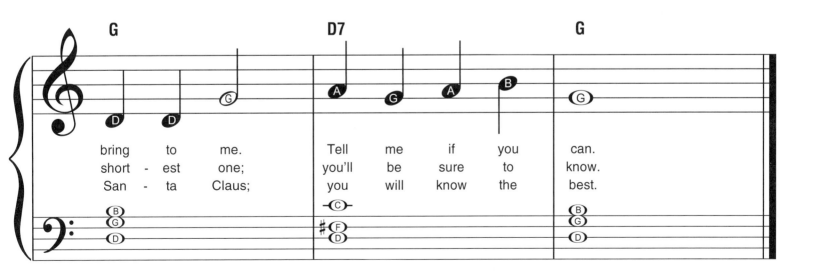

Joy to the World

Words by Isaac Watts
Music by George Frideric Handel
Adapted by Lowell Mason

Joyfully

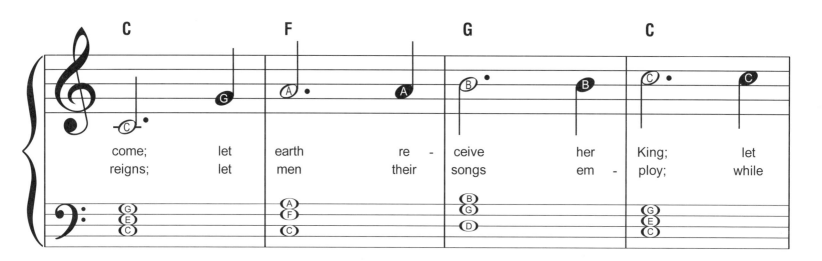

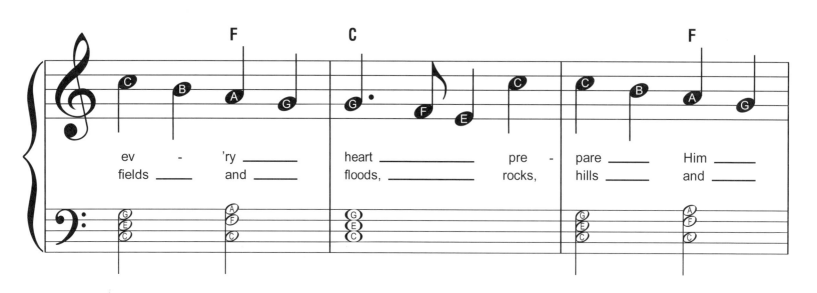

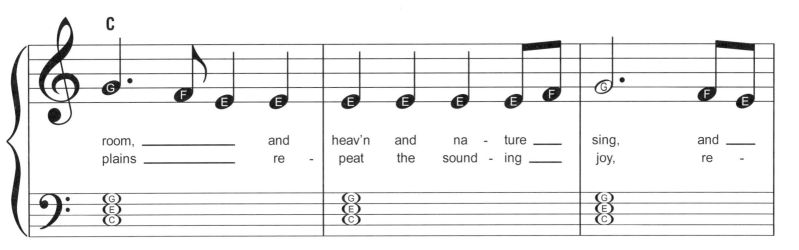

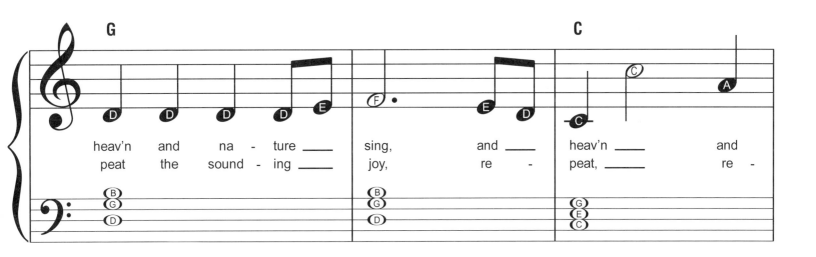

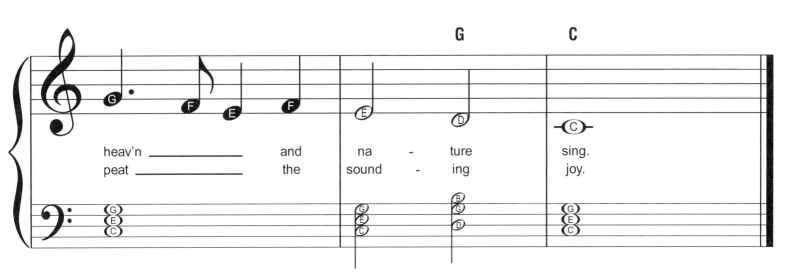

Additional Lyrics

3. No more let sin and sorrow grow,
   Nor thorns infest the ground.
   He comes to make His blessings flow
   Far as the curse is found,
   Far as the curse is found,
   Far as, far as the curse is found.

4. He rules the world with truth and grace,
   And makes the nations prove
   The glories of His righteousness,
   And wonders of His love,
   And wonders of His love,
   And wonders, wonders of His love.

O Christmas Tree

Traditional German Carol

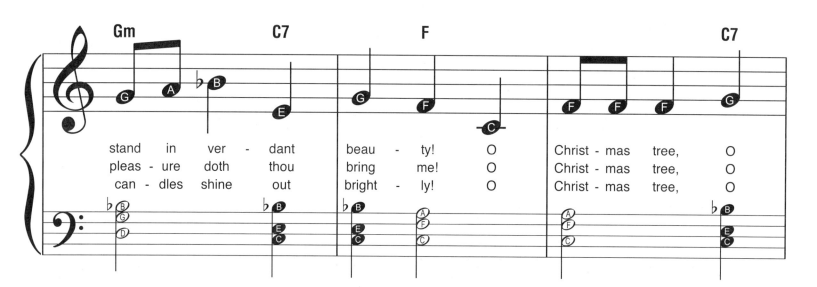

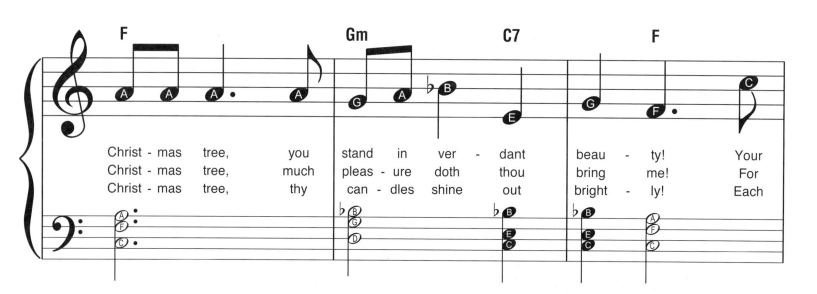

41

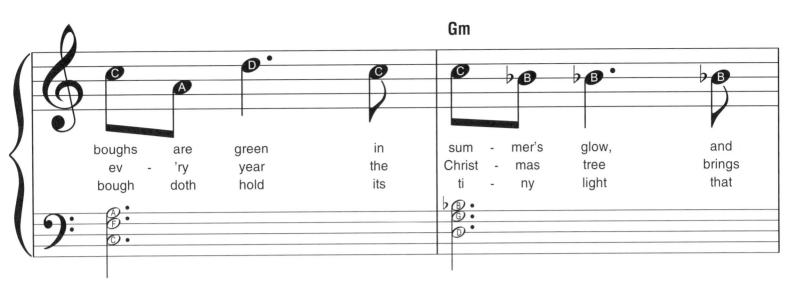

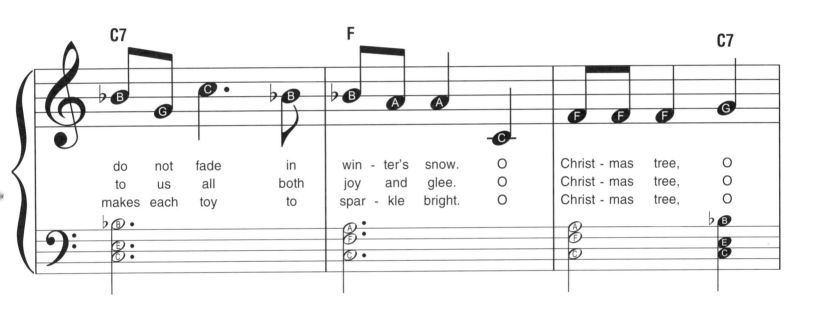

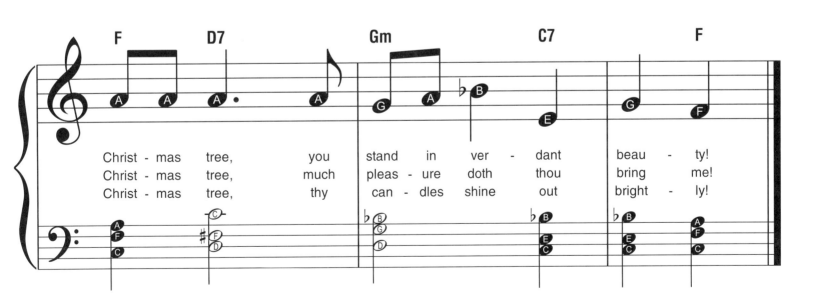

O Come, All Ye Faithful

Music by John Francis Wade
Latin Words translated by Frederick Oakeley

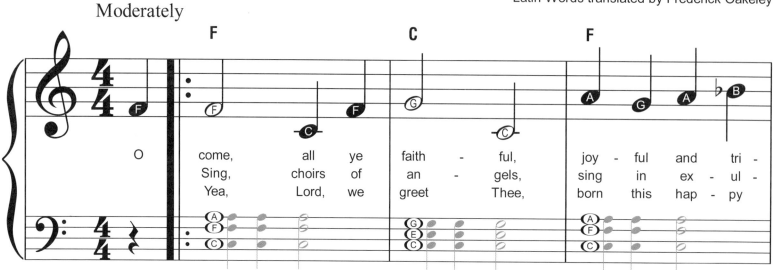

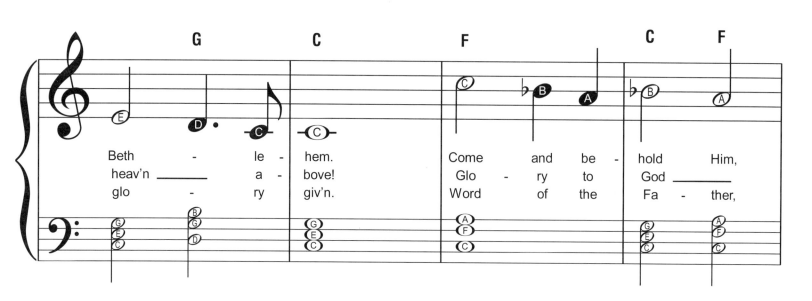

43

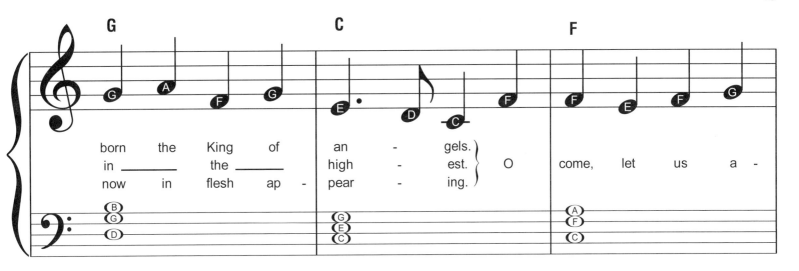

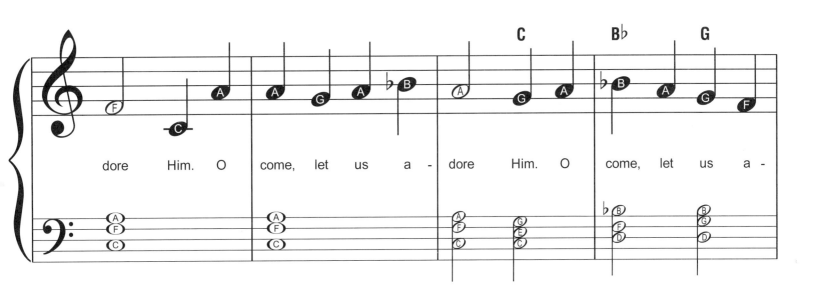

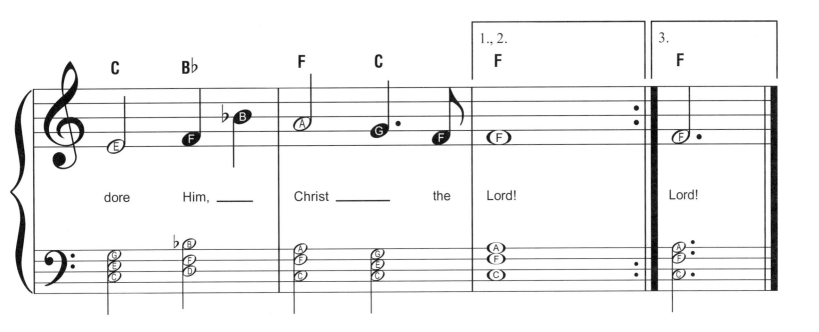

O Come, O Come, Emmanuel

V. 1, 2 translated by John M. Neale
V. 3, 4 translated by Henry S. Coffin
15th Century French Melody
Adapted by Thomas Helmore

Moderately slow

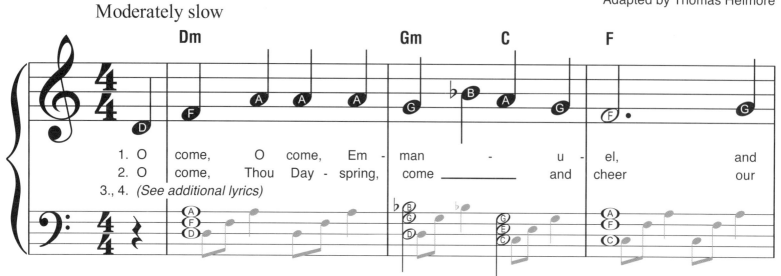

1. O   come,   O come,   Em - man   -   u - el,   and
2. O   come,   Thou Day - spring,   come _____ and   cheer   our
3., 4. *(See additional lyrics)*

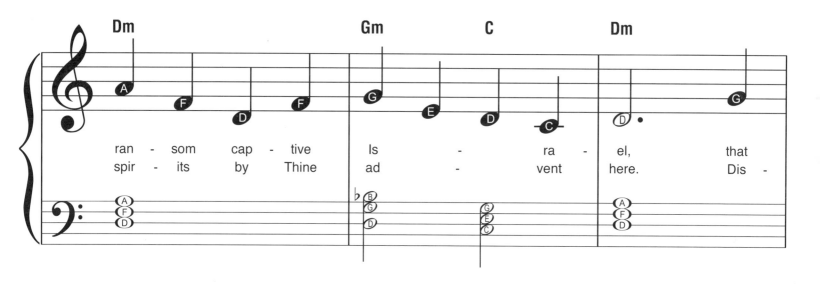

ran - som   cap - tive   Is   -   ra   el,   that
spir - its   by   Thine   ad   -   vent   here.   Dis -

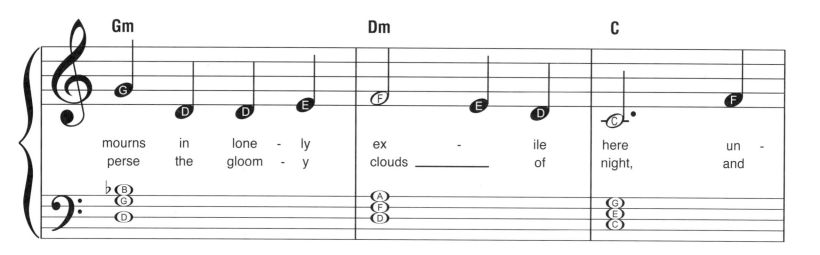

mourns   in   lone - ly   ex   -   ile   here   un -
perse   the   gloom - y   clouds _____ of   night,   and

Refrain

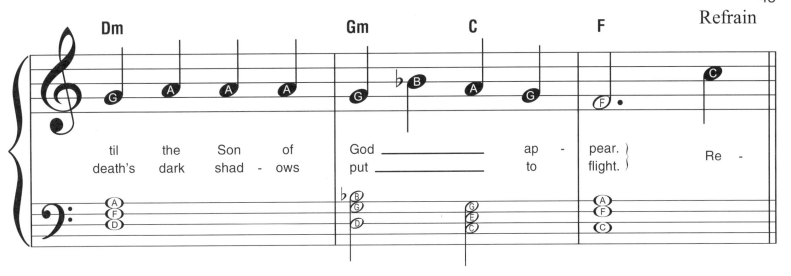

til the Son of God _____ ap - pear.
death's dark shad - ows put _____ to flight. } Re -

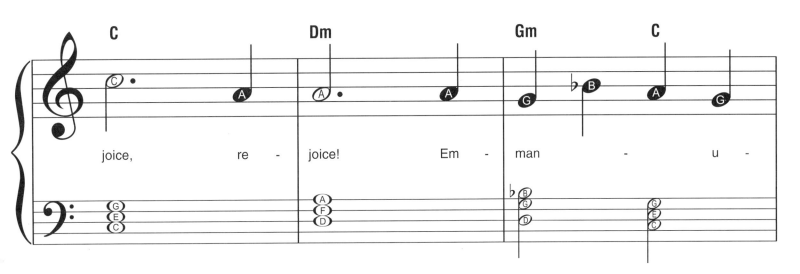

joice, re - joice! Em - man - u -

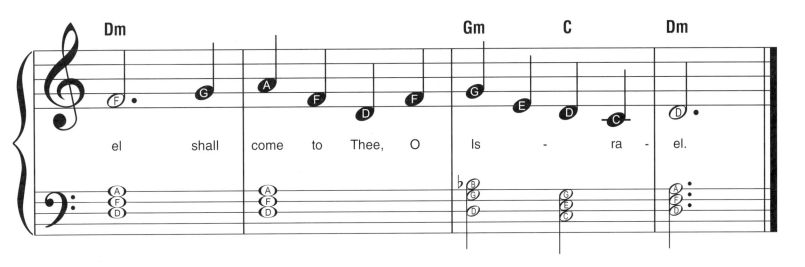

el shall come to Thee, O Is - ra - el.

Additional Lyrics

3. O come, Thou Wisdom from on high,
   And order all things far and nigh.
   To us the path of knowledge show,
   And cause us in her ways to go.
   Refrain

4. O come, Desire of nations, bind
   All people in one heart and mind.
   Bid envy, strife and quarrels cease;
   Fill the whole world with heaven's peace.
   Refrain

O Little Town of Bethlehem

Words by Phillips Brooks
Music by Lewis H. Redner

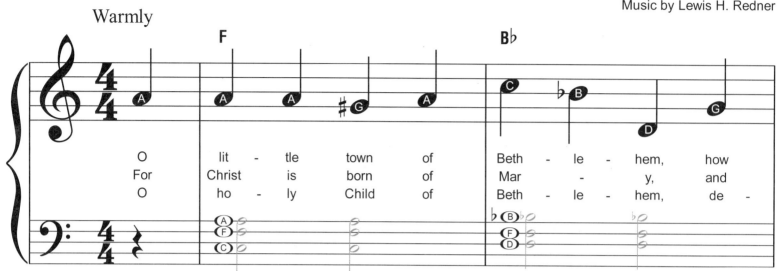

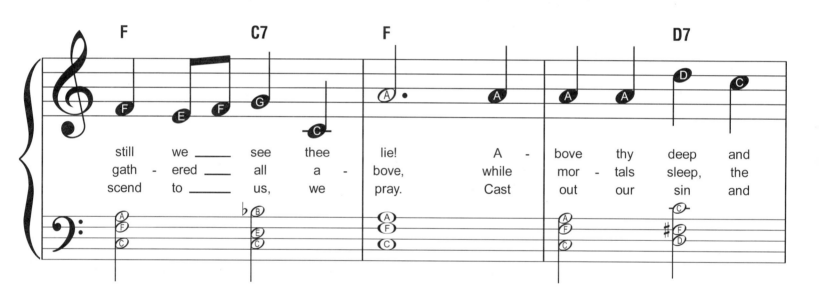

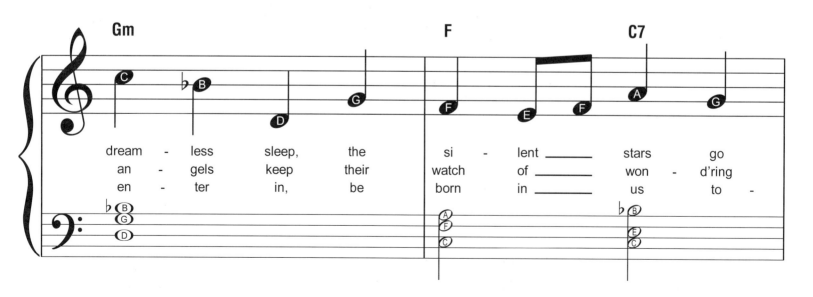

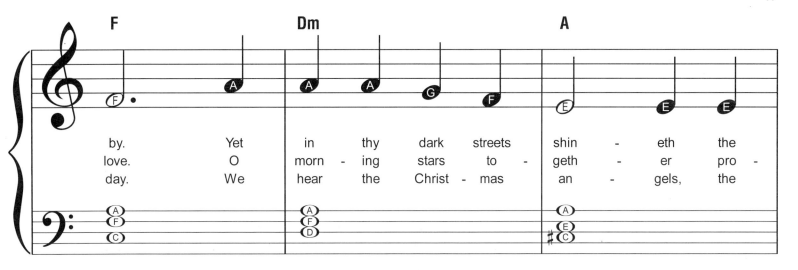

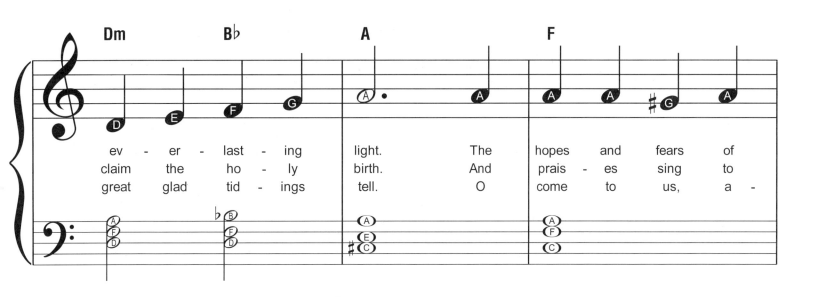

Once in Royal David's City

Words by Cecil F. Alexander
Music by Henry J. Gauntlett

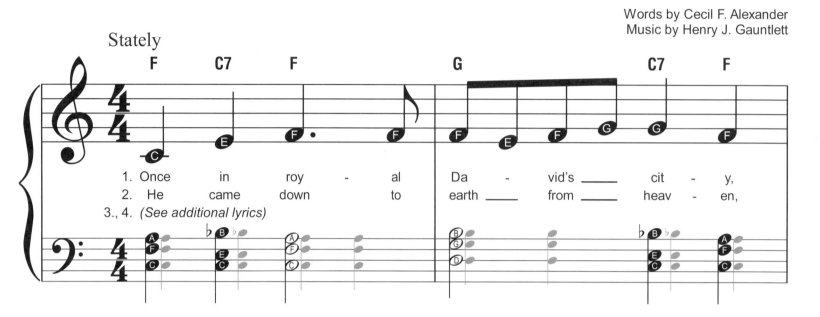

1. Once in roy - al Da - vid's ____ cit - y,
2. He came down to earth ____ from ____ heav - en,
3., 4. *(See additional lyrics)*

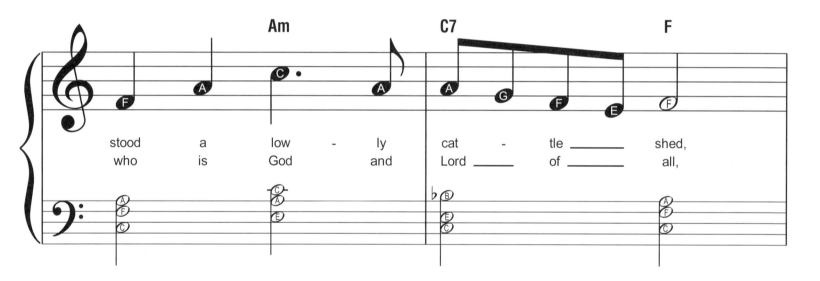

stood a low - ly cat - tle ____ shed,
who is God and Lord ____ of ____ all,

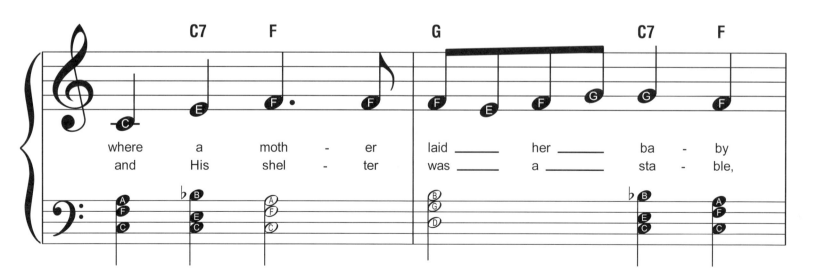

where a moth - er laid ____ her ____ ba - by
and His shel - ter was ____ a ____ sta - ble,

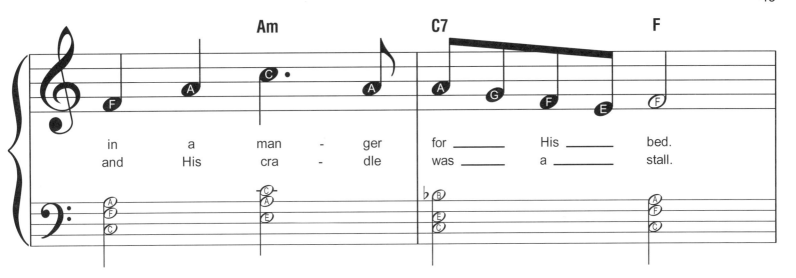

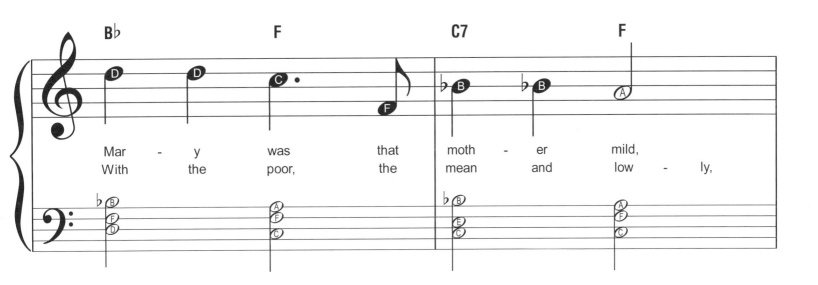

Additional Lyrics

3. Jesus is our childhood's pattern;
Day by day like us He grew.
He was little, weak and helpless;
Tears and smiles, like us, He knew.
And He feeleth for our sadness,
And He shareth in our gladness.

4. And our eyes at last shall see Him,
Through His own redeeming love,
For that Child so dear and gentle
Is our Lord in heav'n above.
And He leads His children on
To the place where He is gone.

Pat-a-Pan
(Willie, Take Your Little Drum)

Words and Music by
Bernard de la Monnoye

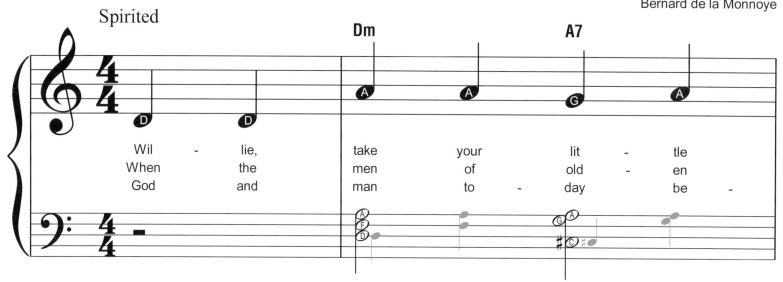

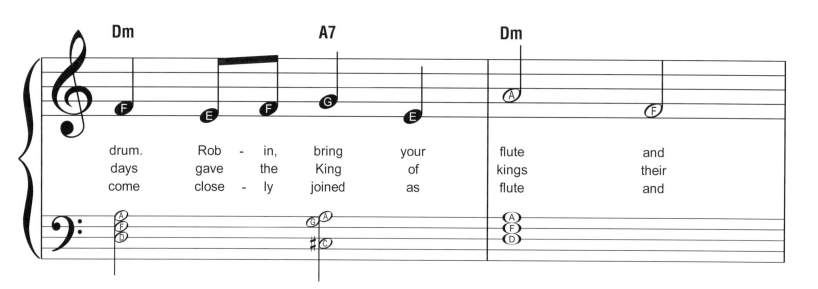

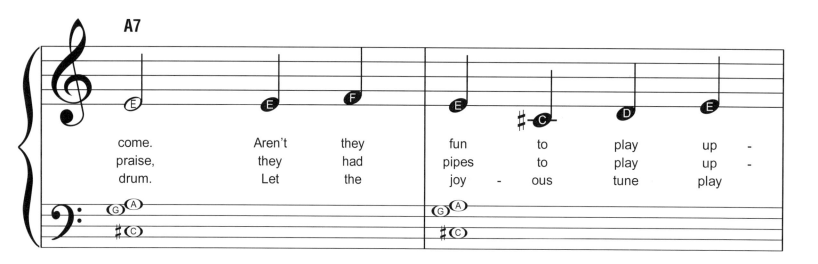

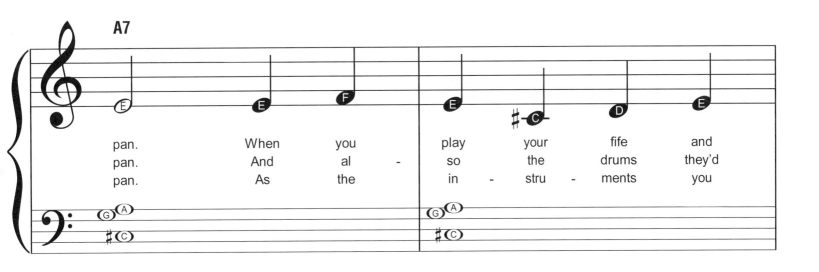

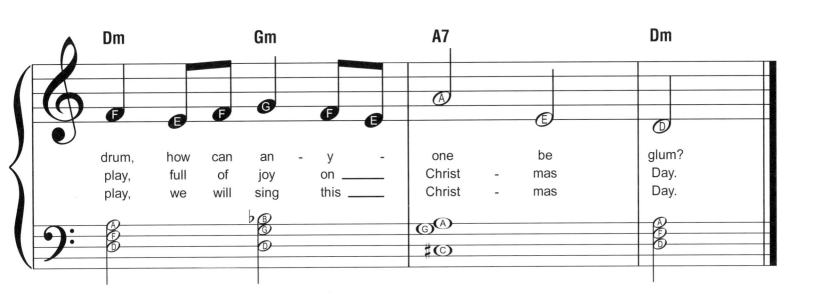

Silent Night

Words by Joseph Mohr
Translated by John F. Young
Music by Franz X. Gruber

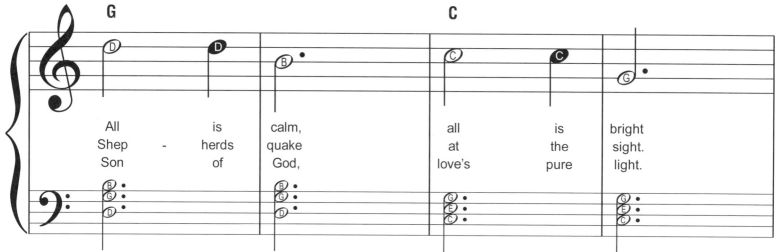

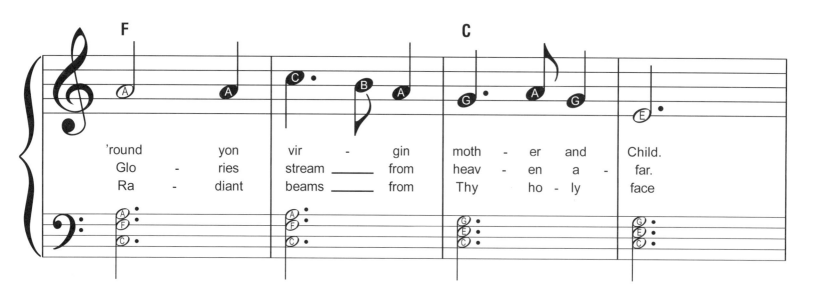

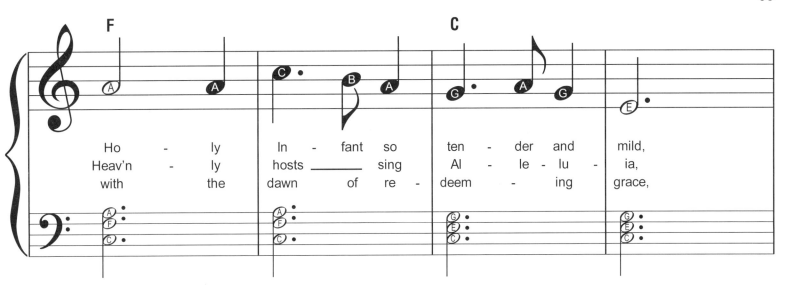

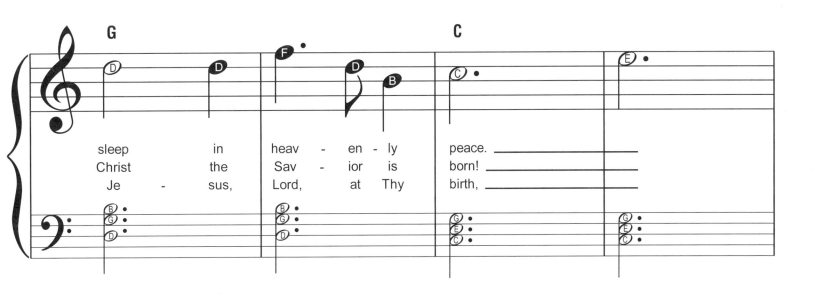

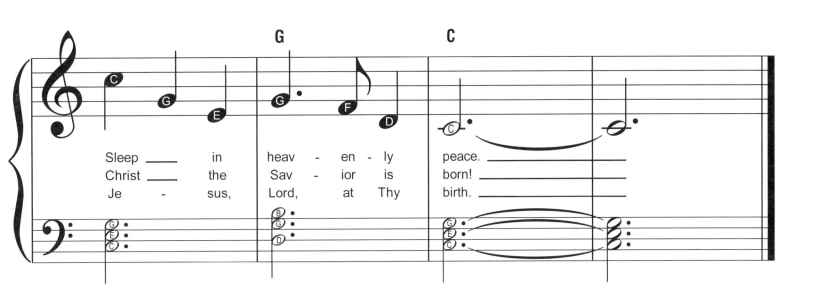

Sing We Now of Christmas

Traditional French Carol

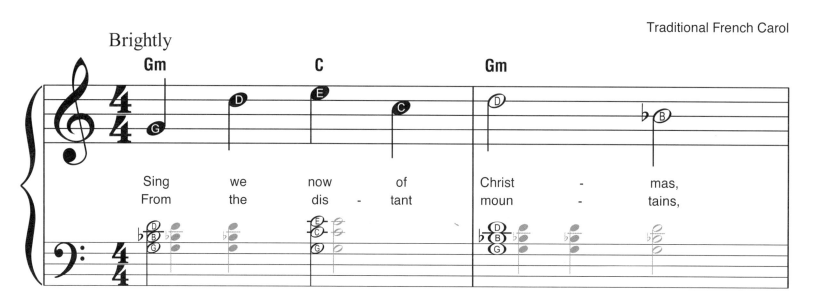

Sing we now of Christ - mas,
From the dis - tant moun - tains,

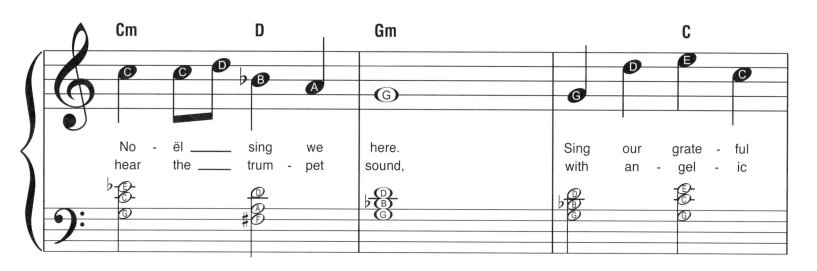

No - ël _____ sing we here.
hear the _____ trum - pet sound,

Sing our grate - ful
with an - gel - ic

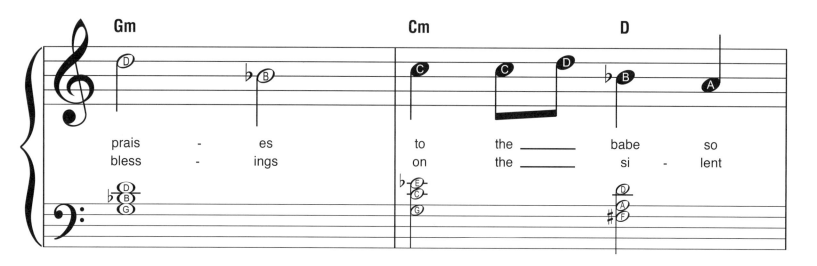

prais - es
bless - ings

to the _____ babe so
on the _____ si - lent

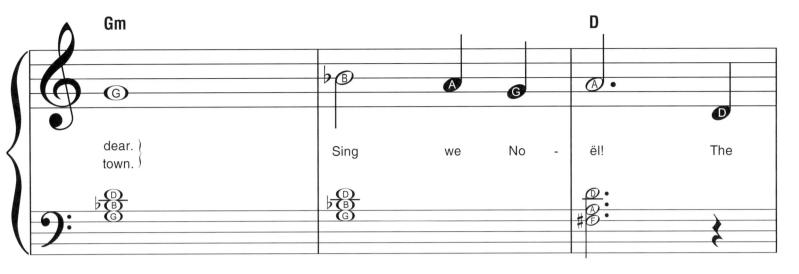

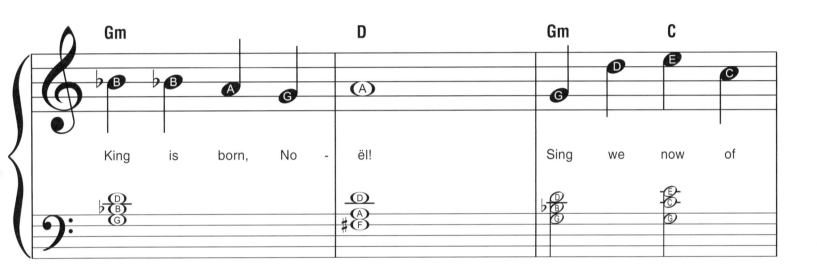

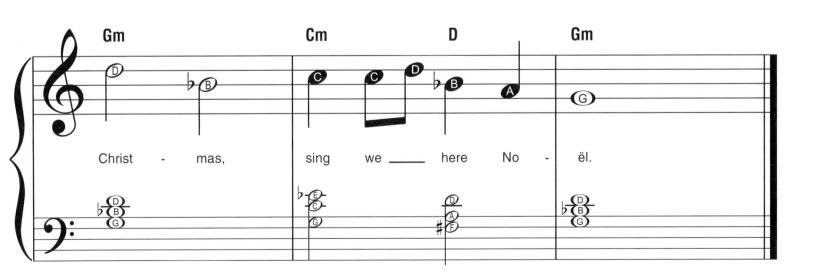

Still, Still, Still

Salzburg Melody, c.1819
Traditional Austrian Text

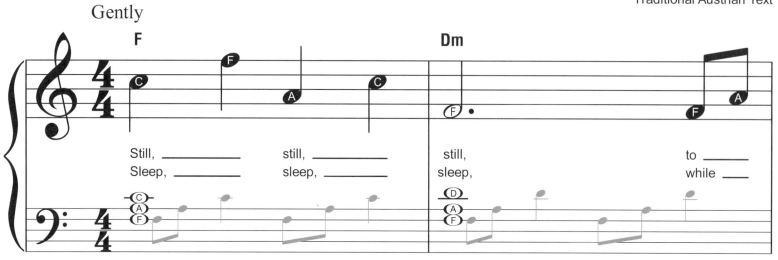

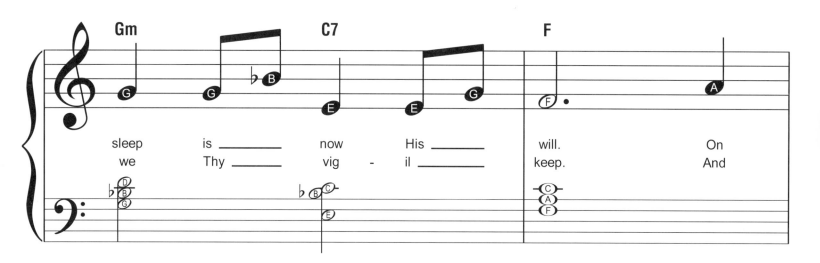

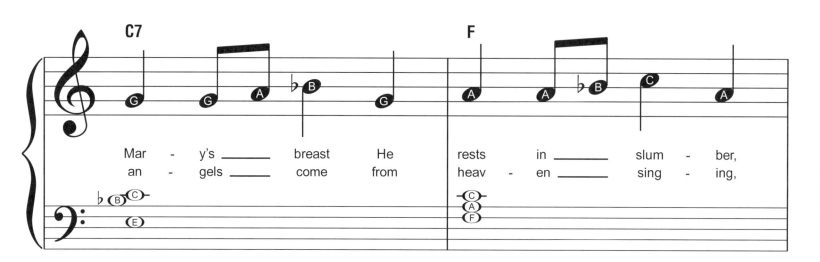

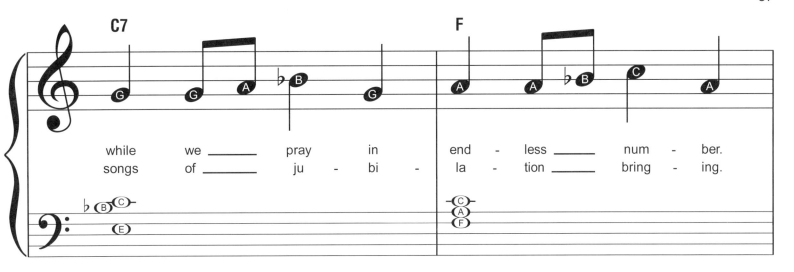

while we _____ pray in end - less _____ num - ber.
songs of _____ ju - bi - la - tion _____ bring - ing.

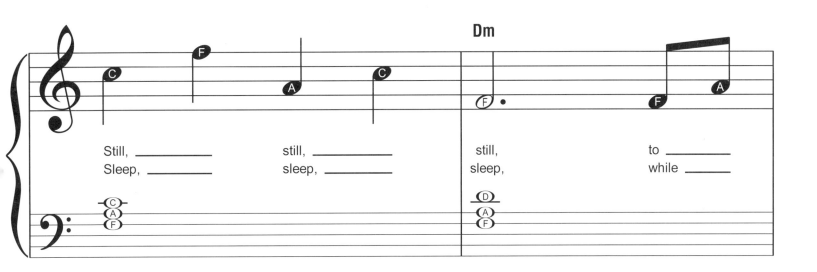

Still, _____ still, _____ still, to _____
Sleep, _____ sleep, _____ sleep, while _____

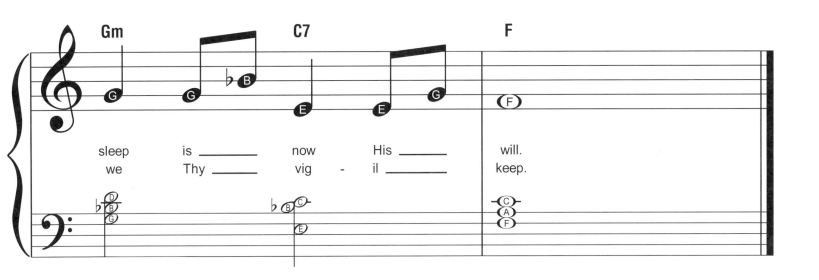

sleep is _____ now His _____ will.
we Thy _____ vig - il _____ keep.

Up on the Housetop

Words and Music by
B.R. Hanby

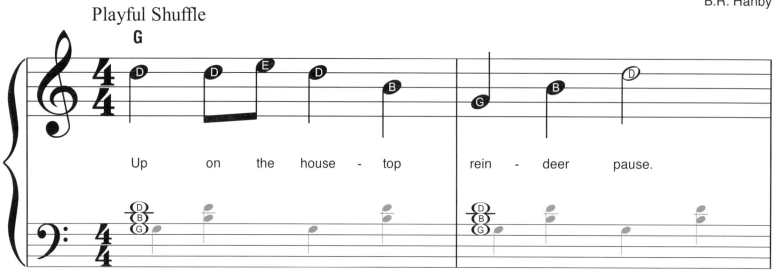

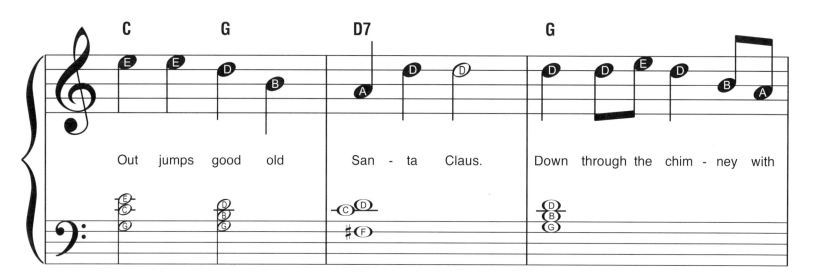

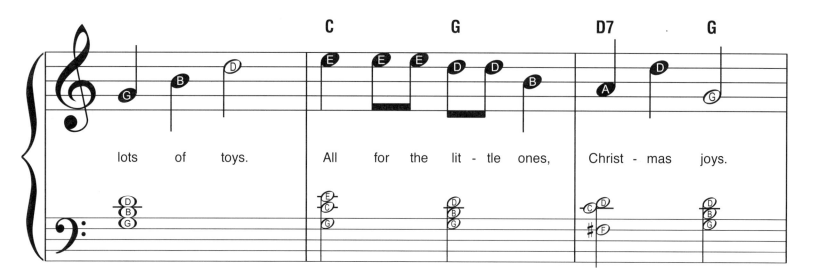

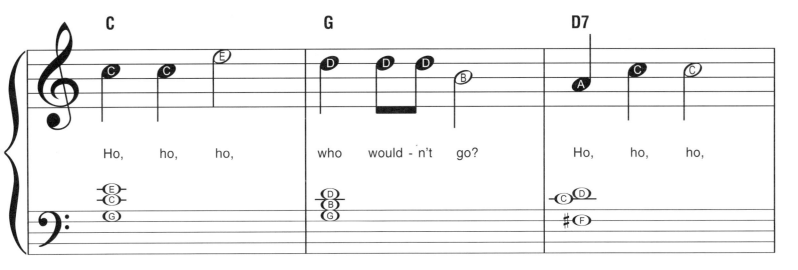

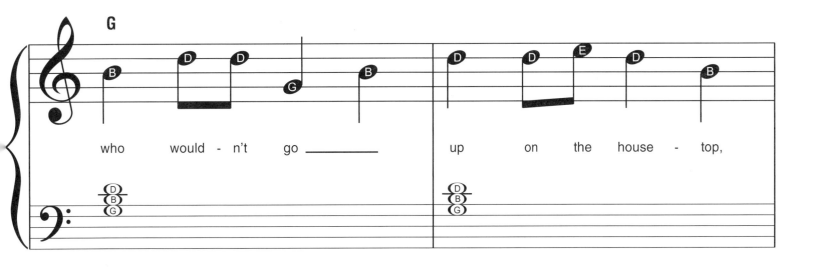

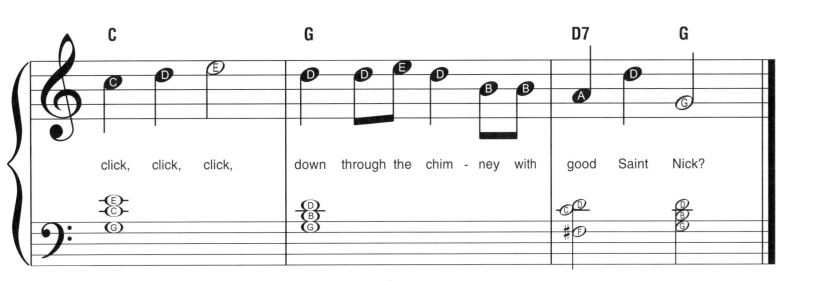

We Three Kings of Orient Are

Words and Music by
John H. Hopkins, Jr.

Moderately fast

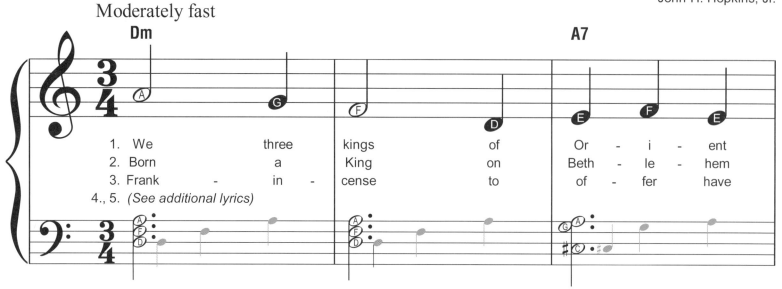

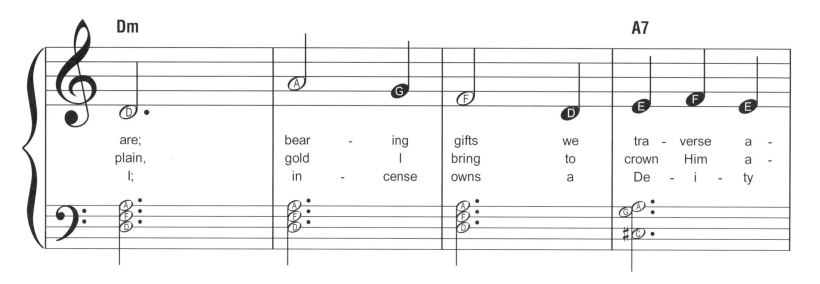

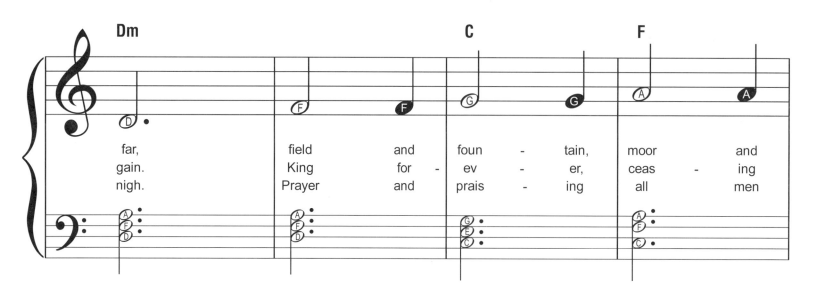

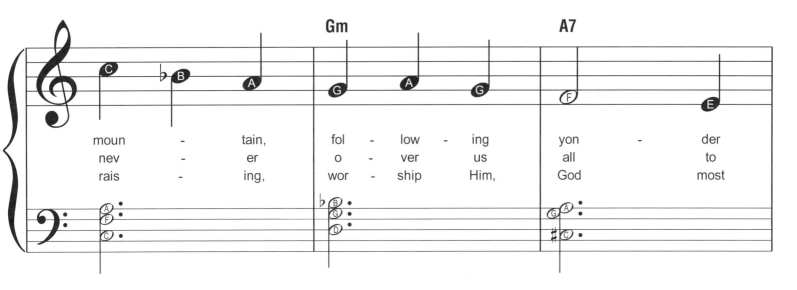

Refrain

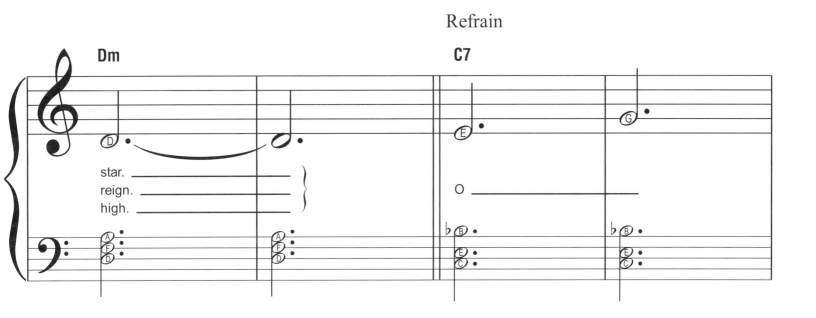

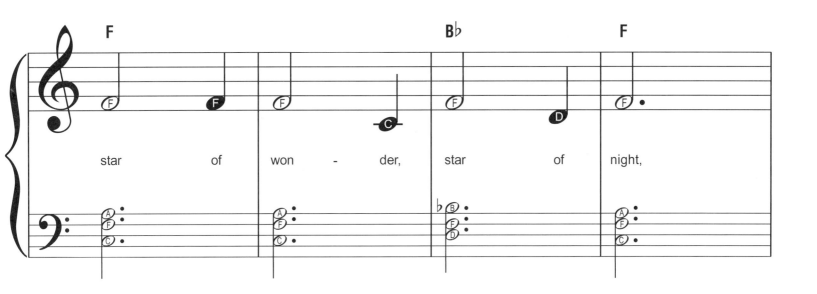

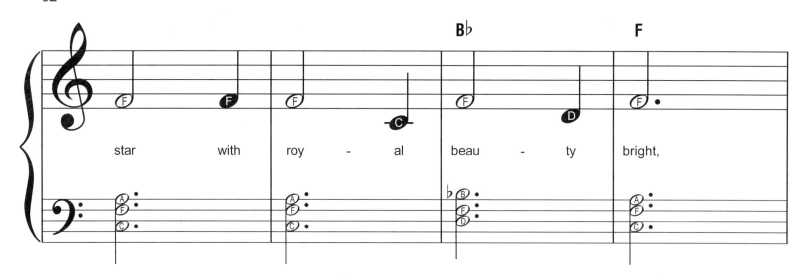

star   with   roy - al   beau - ty   bright,

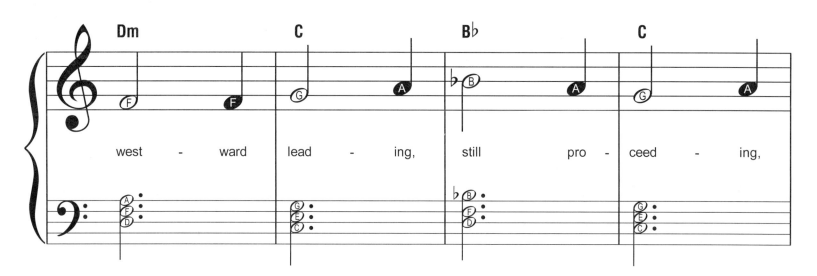

west - ward   lead - ing,   still   pro - ceed - ing,

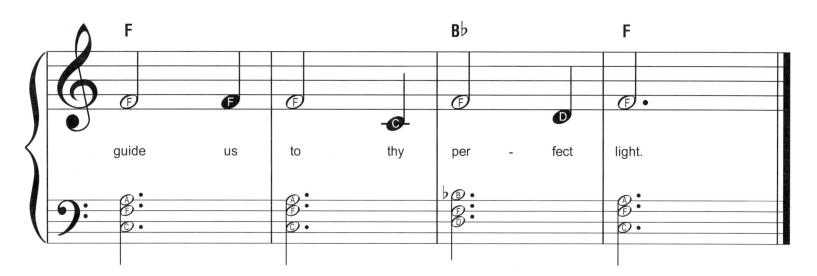

guide   us   to   thy   per - fect   light.

Additional Lyrics

4. Myrrh is mine; its bitter perfume
Breathes a life of gathering gloom;
Sorr'wing, sighing, bleeding, dying,
Sealed in the stone-cold tomb.
Refrain

5. Glorious now, behold Him arise,
King and God and sacrifice.
Alleluia, alleluia
Sounds through the earth and skies.
Refrain

Ukrainian Bell Carol

Traditional
Music by Mykola Leontovych

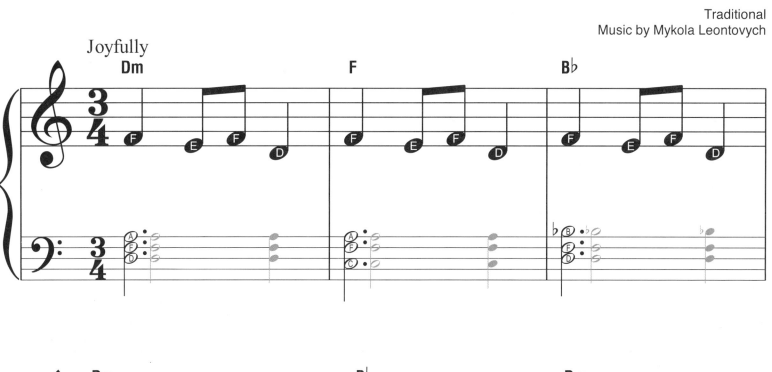

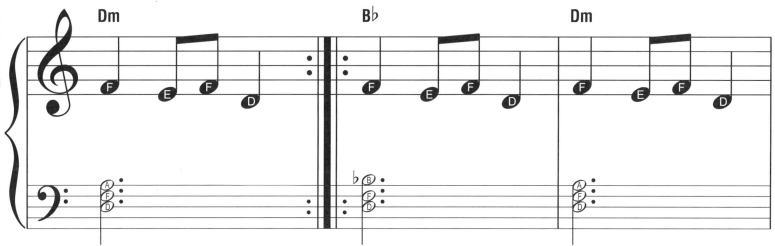

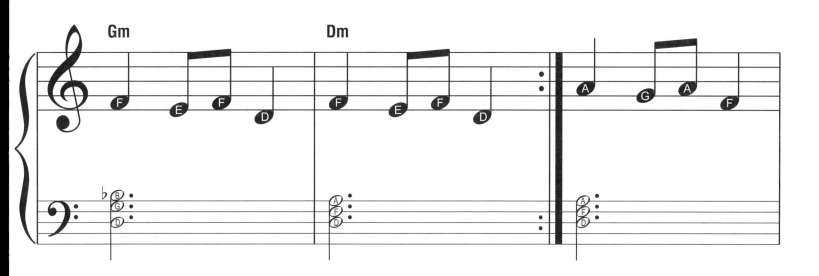

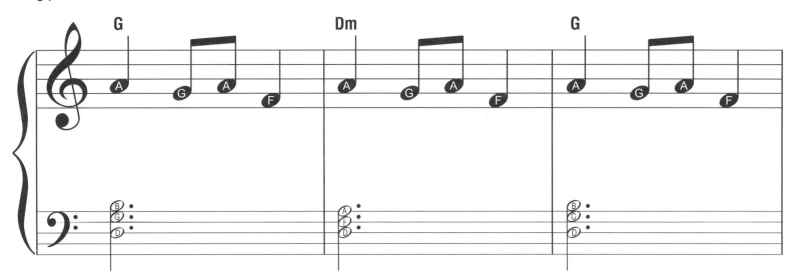

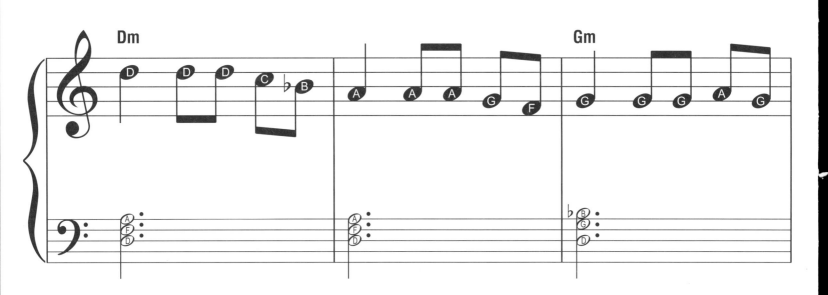

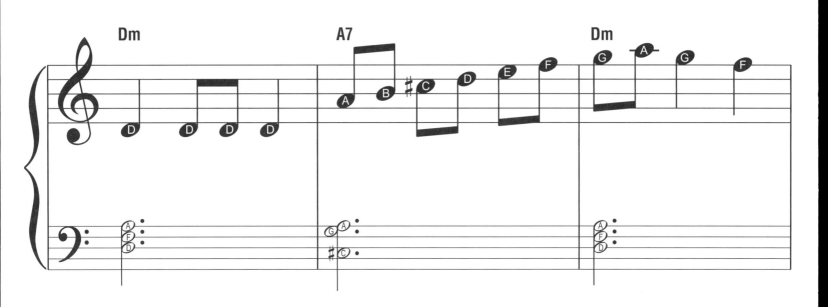

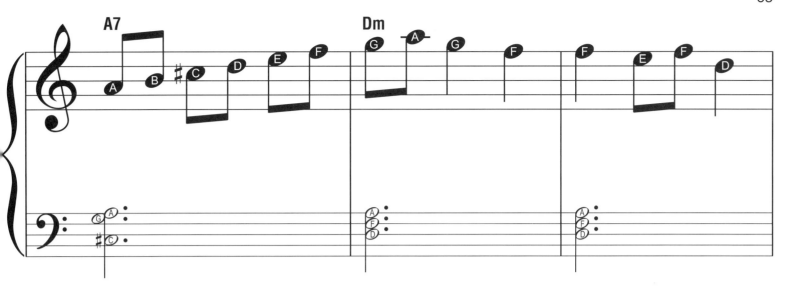

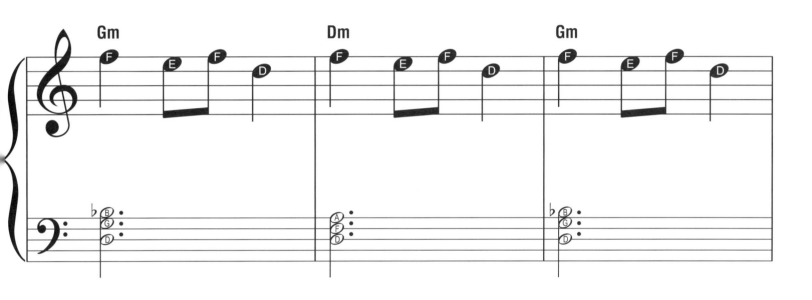

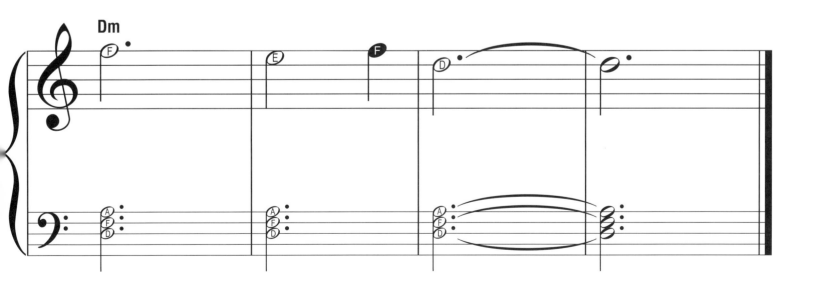

We Wish You a Merry Christmas

Traditional English Folksong

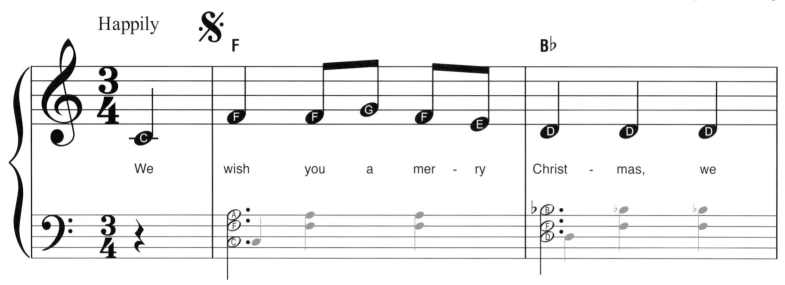

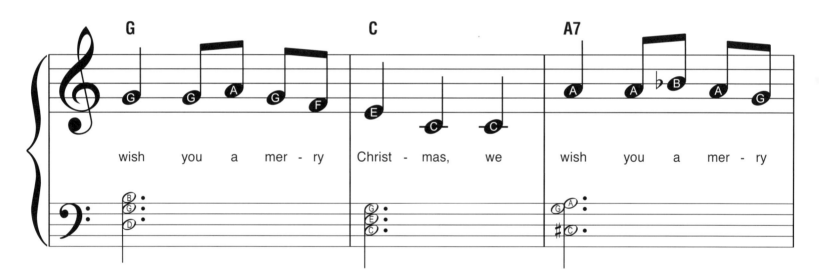

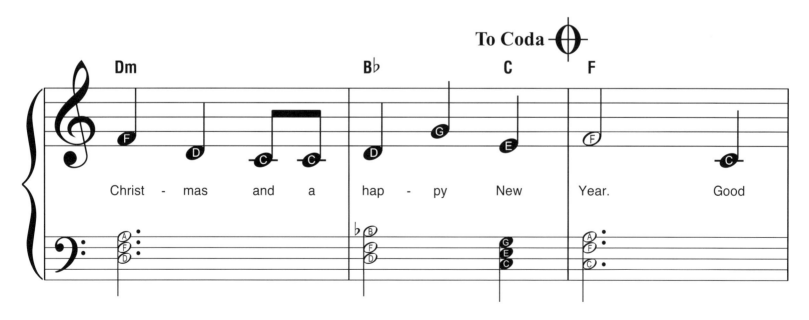

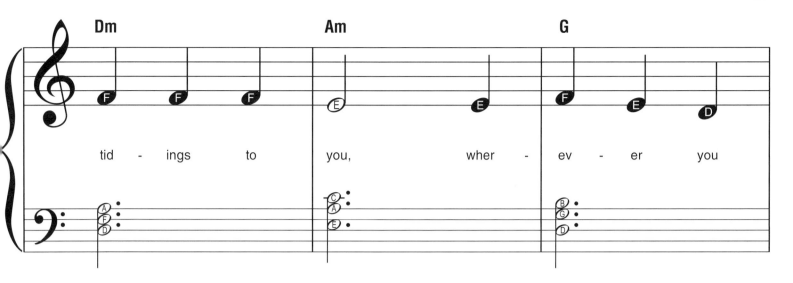

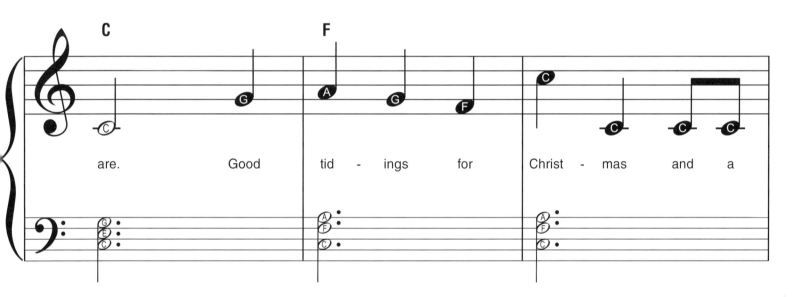

D.S. al Coda
(Return to 𝄋, play to ⊕
and skip to Coda)

CODA

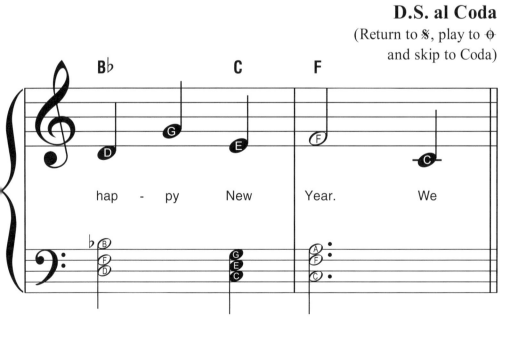

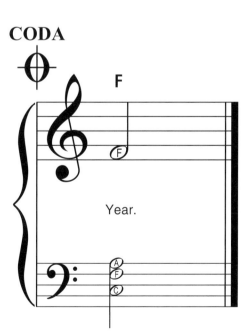

What Child Is This?

Words by William C. Dix
16th Century English Melody

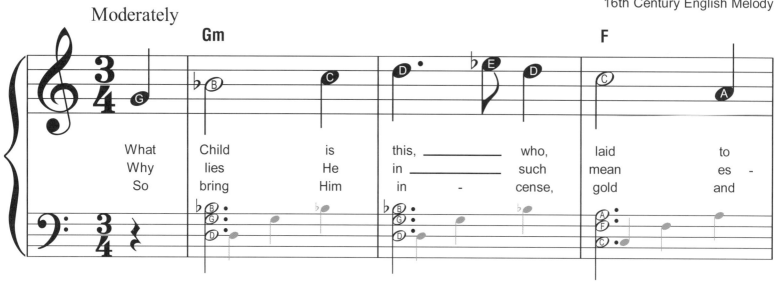

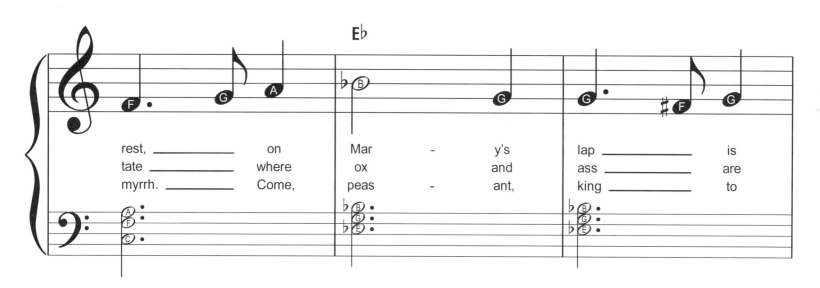

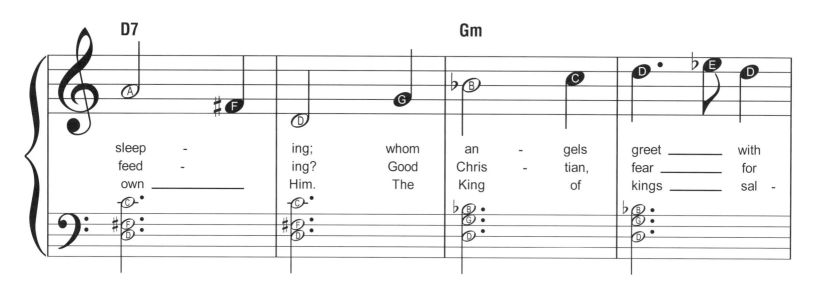

69

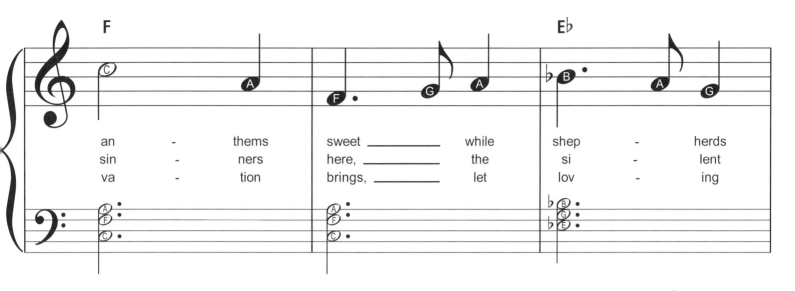

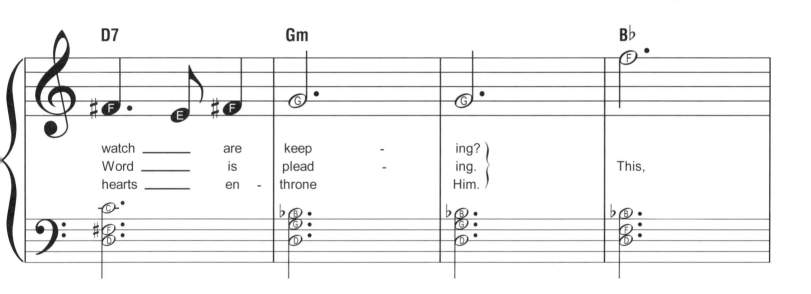

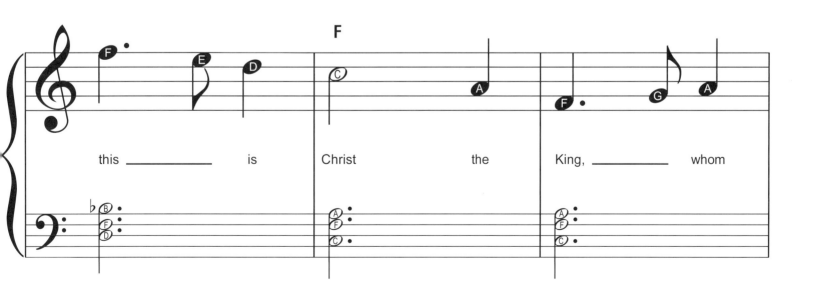

70

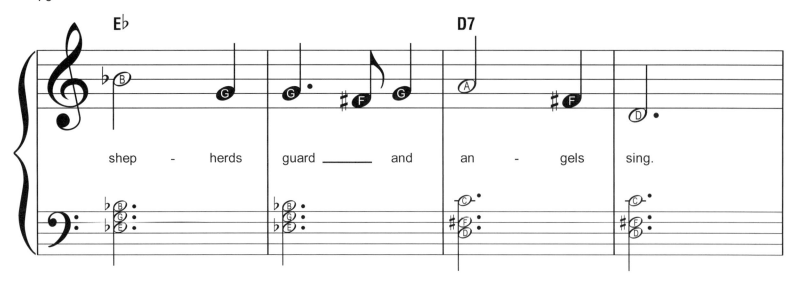

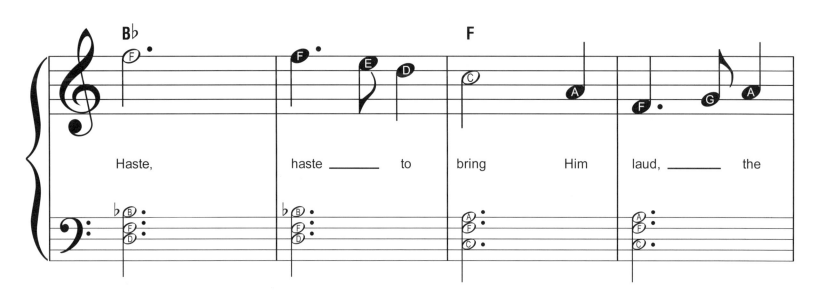

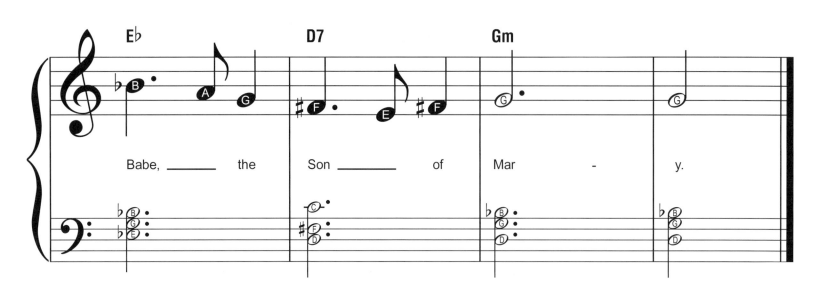

INSTANT Piano Songs

Audio Access Included

The **Instant Piano Songs** series will help you play your favorite songs quickly and easily — whether you use one hand or two! Start with the melody in your right hand, adding basic left-hand chords when you're ready. Letter names inside each note speed up the learning process, and optional rhythm patterns take your playing to the next level. Online backing tracks are also included. Stream or download the tracks using the unique code inside each book, then play along to build confidence and sound great!

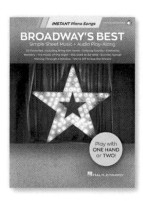

THE BEATLES

All My Loving • Blackbird • Can't Buy Me Love • Eleanor Rigby • Get Back • Here, There and Everywhere • Hey Jude • I Will • Let It Be • Michelle • Nowhere Man • Ob-La-Di, Ob-La-Da • Penny Lane • When I'm Sixty-Four • With a Little Help from My Friends • Yesterday • and more.
00295926 Book/Online Audio $14.99

BROADWAY'S BEST

All I Ask of You • Bring Him Home • Defying Gravity • Don't Cry for Me Argentina • Edelweiss • Memory • The Music of the Night • On My Own • People • Seasons of Love • Send in the Clowns • She Used to Be Mine • Sunrise, Sunset • Tonight • Waving Through a Window • and more.
00323342 Book/Online Audio $14.99

CHRISTMAS CLASSICS

Angels We Have Heard on High • Away in a Manger • Deck the Hall • The First Noel • Good King Wenceslas • Hark! the Herald Angels Sing • Jingle Bells • Jolly Old St. Nicholas • Joy to the World • O Christmas Tree • Up on the Housetop • We Three Kings of Orient Are • We Wish You a Merry Christmas • What Child Is This? • and more.
00348326 Book/Online Audio $14.99

CHRISTMAS STANDARDS

All I Want for Christmas Is You • Christmas Time Is Here • Frosty the Snow Man • Grown-Up Christmas List • A Holly Jolly Christmas • I'll Be Home for Christmas • Jingle Bell Rock • The Little Drummer Boy • Mary, Did You Know? • Merry Christmas, Darling • Rudolph the Red-Nosed Reindeer • White Christmas • and more.
00294854 Book/Online Audio $14.99

CLASSICAL THEMES

Canon (Pachelbel) • Für Elise (Beethoven) • Jesu, Joy of Man's Desiring (Bach) • Jupiter (Holst) • Lullaby (Brahms) • Pomp and Circumstance (Elgar) • Spring (Vivaldi) • Symphony No. 9, Fourth Movement ("Ode to Joy") (Beethoven) • and more.
00283826 Book/Online Audio $14.99

DISNEY FAVORITES

Beauty and the Beast • Can You Feel the Love Tonight • Chim Chim Cher-ee • Colors of the Wind • A Dream Is a Wish Your Heart Makes • Friend Like Me • How Far I'll Go • It's a Small World • Kiss the Girl • Lava • Let It Go • Mickey Mouse March • Part of Your World • Reflection • Remember Me (Ernesto de la Cruz) • A Whole New World • You'll Be in My Heart (Pop Version) • and more.
00283720 Book/Online Audio $14.99

HITS OF 2010-2019 – INSTANT PIANO SONGS

All About That Bass (Meghan Trainor) • All of Me (John Legend) • Can't Stop the Feeling (Justin Timberlake) • Happy (Pharrell Williams) • Hey, Soul Sister (Train) • Just the Way You Are (Bruno Mars) • Rolling in the Deep (Adele) • Shallow (Lady Gaga & Bradley Cooper) • Shake It Off (Taylor Swift) • Shape of You (Ed Sheeran) • and more.
00345364 Book/Online Audio $14.99

MOVIE SONGS

As Time Goes By • City of Stars • Endless Love • Hallelujah • I Will Always Love You • Laura • Moon River • My Heart Will Go on (Love Theme from 'Titanic') • Over the Rainbow • Singin' in the Rain • Skyfall • Somewhere Out There • Stayin' Alive • Tears in Heaven • Unchained Melody • Up Where We Belong • The Way We Were • What a Wonderful World • and more.
00283718 Book/Online Audio $14.99

POP HITS

All of Me • Chasing Cars • Despacito • Feel It Still • Havana • Hey, Soul Sister • Ho Hey • I'm Yours • Just Give Me a Reason • Love Yourself • Million Reasons • Perfect • Riptide • Shake It Off • Stay with Me • Thinking Out Loud • Viva La Vida • What Makes You Beautiful • and more.
00283825 Book/Online Audio $14.99

SONGS FOR KIDS – INSTANT PIANO SONGS

Do-Re-Mi • Hakuna Matata • It's a Small World • On Top of Spaghetti • Puff the Magic Dragon • The Rainbow Connection • SpongeBob SquarePants Theme Song • Take Me Out to the Ball Game • Tomorrow • The Wheels on the Bus • Won't You Be My Neighbor? (It's a Beautiful Day in the Neighborhood) • You Are My Sunshine • and more.
00323352 Book/Online Audio $14.99

www.halleonard.com

SUPER EASY SONGBOOK

It's super easy! This series features accessible arrangements for piano, with simple right-hand melody, letter names inside each note, and basic left-hand chord diagrams. Perfect for players of all ages!

THE BEATLES
00198161.................................. $14.99

BEETHOVEN
00345533.................................. $9.99

BEST SONGS EVER
00329877.................................. $14.99

BROADWAY
00193871.................................. $14.99

JOHNNY CASH
00287524.................................. $9.99

CHRISTMAS CAROLS
00277955.................................. $14.99

CHRISTMAS SONGS
00236850.................................. $14.99

CLASSIC ROCK
00287526.................................. $14.99

CLASSICAL
00194693.................................. $14.99

COUNTRY
00285257.................................. $14.99

DISNEY
00199558.................................. $14.99

BILLIE EILISH
00346515.................................. $10.99

FOUR CHORD SONGS
00249533.................................. $14.99

FROZEN COLLECTION
00334069.................................. $10.99

GEORGE GERSHWIN
00345536.................................. $9.99

GOSPEL
00285256.................................. $14.99

HIT SONGS
00194367.................................. $14.99

HYMNS
00194659.................................. $14.99

JAZZ STANDARDS
00233687.................................. $14.99

BILLY JOEL
00329996.................................. $9.99

ELTON JOHN
00298762.................................. $9.99

KIDS' SONGS
00198009.................................. $14.99

LEAN ON ME
00350593.................................. $9.99

THE LION KING
00303511.................................. $9.99

ANDREW LLOYD WEBBER
00249580.................................. $14.99

MOVIE SONGS
00233670.................................. $14.99

POP SONGS FOR KIDS
00346809.................................. $14.99

POP STANDARDS
00233770.................................. $14.99

QUEEN
00294889.................................. $9.99

ED SHEERAN
00287525.................................. $9.99

SIMPLE SONGS
00329906.................................. $14.99

STAR WARS
00345560.................................. $9.99

TAYLOR SWIFT
00323195.................................. $9.99

THREE CHORD SONGS
00249664.................................. $14.99

TOP HITS
00300405.................................. $9.99

Prices, contents and availability subject to change without notice.

Disney Characters and Artwork TM & © 2019 Disney

HAL•LEONARD®

www.halleonard.com